A SURVIVAL BOOK

5 Birds in the Balance

Survival Books are published in close association with Anglia Television's Natural History Unit who make the 'Survival' series of television documentaries on wildlife.

SURVIVAL BOOKS

Edited by Colin Willock

ALREADY PUBLISHED

*

The Private Life of the Rabbit
R. M. Lockley

Birds of Prey
Philip Brown

Living with Deer
Richard Prior

Town Fox, Country Fox
Brian Vesey-Fitzgerald

A SURVIVAL BOOK ON BIRDS

Slaughtered wedge-tailed eagles in Australia

Birds in the Balance

PHILIP BROWN

A SURVIVAL BOOK

Editor Colin Willock

ANDRE DEUTSCH

FIRST PUBLISHED 1966 BY
ANDRE DEUTSCH LIMITED
105 GREAT RUSSELL STREET
LONDON WCI
COPYRIGHT © 1966 BY PHILIP BROWN
ALL RIGHTS RESERVED
PRINTED IN GREAT BRITAIN BY
EBENEZER BAYLIS AND SON LTD
THE TRINITY PRESS
WORCESTER AND LONDON

To

JOHN ANDERTON

Good sportsman; good conservationist
and a very good friend

Author's Note

This book is an introduction to some of the problems – and they are legion – of conserving wild birds. If the emphasis is on western Europe (especially Great Britain and the Netherlands) and the USA., the theme is a universal one and could often, I believe, be applied to other animals as well as birds.

We cannot hope to save rare wild creatures unless we are prepared to give them reasonable living-room. Even then, the habitat must be managed, some plants and creatures must be controlled and adequate steps must be taken to prevent human interference or exploitation.

We all know that space is at a premium. Something like half the human population of the world is undernourished, though a percentage of the remainder apparently risk their health by over-eating and food-surpluses are not unknown in some countries. In the way of progress, the twentieth century, for all its conceit, has not exactly hit the jackpot.

The view is sometimes expressed that the preservation of birds and other wildlife is a luxury we cannot afford if we are to raise our own standards of living. But who wants to live in a desert, anyway?

I hope that this book will interest those who enjoy birds, whether they sit and watch them or shoot and eat them. The hunter is a great ally of conservation if he behaves himself reasonably and practises tolerance; so is the bird-watcher, subject to exactly the same conditions.

PHILIP BROWN

Everton, Bedfordshire
August, 1965.

Foreword

Bird books have been rolling off the conveyor belt in increasing numbers ever since I was a small schoolboy. In those days I was the only boy in the school who was interested in birds, and in consequence I was regarded by one and all as a chump. Today there is probably not a school in the country without its natural history society, bird group, or whatever it may be called. The spectacular explosion of public interest in birds and the countryside since the war accounts for the mounting spate of books. And it is certainly time that we had another book from Philip Brown.

Any book on birds by Philip Brown commands attention. He is a prince of ornithologists, a fearless commando among bird protectors, and an inspiration to that massive group in the naturalist movement, the bird people. But above all, and let me underline it, Philip Brown is a bird man who has his head clear about his objectives, and in this he belongs to a minority. Furthermore, in having his head clear *and* in proclaiming his ideas confidently to naturalists at large, he is associated only with a handful.

In this sense I welcome *Birds in the Balance*. The heartening thing is that it is not another book just about birds. It is about people. It is about what people have done about birds. It is really about us, us frightful bird people, of every sub-species and phoney variation, and of the splendid muddles we have managed to contrive, or allowed others to perpetrate, in the grand cause of keeping Britain a good bird place for our descendants. But this book also gives a stirring account of the wonderful things that have been done, particularly since the war. This first opportunity of reading the whole history of bird protection in Britain must be a landmark for the cause and serve to give encouragement to all in the future.

This is the first book by a distinguished ornithologist which insistently uses the term 'conservationist', at the expense of such frivolous designations as 'bird lover'. Is a good farmer a cow lover or a pig lover? Of course not. Yet nobody criticises the farmer if he builds up a fine herd for breeding, showing, or cropping, and is not a sentimentalist who refuses to face facts. But the natural history movement is rife with people who refuse to face facts. With many of them I confess I have some sympathy; in their ignorance they are mostly honest. But with experienced naturalists who know and understand the facts, yet who funk the necessity of challenging sentiment when seeking support for conservation, or worse still who exploit sentiment for the advantage of their wildlife professions, for these people I have absolutely no time at all.

In Anglia's 'Survival' series on ITV we set our face against 'pandering' from the outset. We strive to explain the techniques and problems of conservation. And we have been encouraged to feel that we have established a new approach and standard in the presentation of natural history on television. We may be forgiven for persevering with some enthusiasm when 'Survival' wins a larger audience than 'Top of the Pops'. And this came about we believe through directness, frankness, and no inconvenient facts being swept under the carpet. Now *Birds in the Balance* by Philip Brown hoists the same standard of realism and truth in the field of natural history literature, and we are privileged therefore to acclaim this notable author as a pioneer.

This book by Philip Brown, when widely read – as it surely will be – will certainly help the majority to comprehend the problems of bird conservation and encourage supporters of the countryside, whatever their particular interests, to appreciate that their objectives can be reconciled.

Stansted, Essex   AUBREY BUXTON

Contents

Illustrations

Introduction

There are something like 8,600 different species of birds in the world. Nobody knows the total numbers involved but the figure almost certainly runs into billions. Some of the species are rare; two or three per cent of the total number of species we know of are on the edge of complete extermination. Several hundred more species are so rare, or so specialised in their habits, that their future is uncertain. At a rough estimate ten per cent of the total of 8,600 species need help of some sort or another if they are to survive. But the total populations of these 800 odd rarer species represent an insignificant fraction of the countless billions of birds in existence today.

More than half the 8,600 species are common and at least a quarter are abundant by any standards. There are far more birds which are a nuisance to us in one way or another, real or imaginary, than there are rare ones in danger of extinction. One of the first known birds, the fossil Archaeopteryx, is believed to have flourished considerably more than 100 million years ago, which is so far back in time that the human mind cannot possibly comprehend it. And long before primitive man first shambled about the earth innumerable species of birds had become extinct by the normal processes of evolution. If man had never evolved there would today almost certainly have been some species which would have been common but others which were rare – relict species, if you like, which would have been doomed to extinction through the ordinary processes of natural selection and the survival of the fittest.

Birds are only a very small part of the complex pattern of life. No single creature could survive on its own. Man himself, for all his twentieth-century self-confidence, is a part of this living pattern. He is as much dependent upon it as the sparrowhawk and the conger-eel, the locust and the lion, the sequoia and the oak, the blueberry and the pampas grass. It is not given to man alone to destroy. Yet through his superior intelligence he wields powers possessed by no other creature on earth.

Man has been slaughtering animals far too long to bother us. Because he must live, he has killed them for food; he has killed them because they were dangerous and would otherwise kill him; and he has killed them in an effort to protect his domestic livestock and his crops. He has also hunted animals for the sport of it; he has captured and caged them for his pleasure and pride. He has used their skins or feathers for clothing and adornment. He has seldom missed an opportunity to exploit other creatures for his own profit, even to the extent of killing the goose which lays the golden egg. No other living creature has been so extravagant, so knowledgeably careless, so wasteful, so callous and so self-indulgent as man. On this happy note the author and the reader are able to introduce themselves to one another.

1 Why Conserve?

Why all this modern fuss about conserving birds and other wild life, anyway? Take the Californian condor, for instance. One of the largest land birds in the world, it is also indisputably amongst the finest birds of prey. Today it survives only in a relatively small area in the extreme west of the United States of America. The total number of individuals in existence at the present time is around or a little above fifty. Young birds do not breed until their sixth year. The chances of ultimate survival are negligible unless the numbers can not only be maintained but increased. If one could mark off what would be a vast area, leaving it largely unchanged and undisturbed, there would be every prospect that the Californian condor would successfully hold its own. This being obviously impossible, the National Audubon Society, amongst others, is desperately engaged upon publicising the plight of the species and resisting, so far as it can, any developments in the area which are not essential and which would be unfavourable to the few remaining birds.

But the practical reader may well ask: How much poorer would the world be today if we lost the Californian condor? How many amongst the huge and exploding world population have the slightest chance of seeing this magnificent bird of prey even if they wanted to? And what tiny fractional percentage even want to? We have already lost at least seventy different kinds of birds in the last two or three hundred years. Who is the poorer for not being able to see a living dodo, great auk or passenger pigeon? At least in the case of a few of these species which have vanished, there are stuffed specimens which can be studied in

museums, whilst in the case of a number of others which are very likely
to become extinct before the end of the century, there will probably be
many more mounted specimens – not to mention skins for scientific
study – available in museums scattered over a much wider area of the
globe than that ever occupied by the living birds themselves.

This is the naïve, negative approach which is often trotted out by
those who find any plans of their own thwarted by those responsible
for wild life interests. Much the same arguments could be advanced in
respect of the Mona Lisa or St Paul's Cathedral in London, or St Peter's
in Rome, or the Grand Canyon in Arizona or the Victoria Falls in East
Africa. Even the most ardent traveller with well-lined pockets would be
unlikely to see all five of these things in his lifetime. Amongst the living,
not one person in ten thousand will see a single one of them. A very
large proportion of those who will never see any of them would be unlikely to thank you if you gave them the opportunity.

Yet St Paul's Cathedral is not only an historical part of the British
heritage: it is also a money-spinner. It helps to attract tourists. It is
one of the things which has given Britain much-needed dollars. It is
highly probable that, viewed simply on a sordid commercial basis, the
Cathedral has repaid its original cost over and over again. The interest in rare or strange, beautiful or magnificent birds and animals may
be no less valuable, even from the purely commercial angle, in the long
run. A striking example of the enormous public sympathy in matters of
this kind was demonstrated when a single pair of ospreys – large fish-
eating hawks – began nesting again in Scotland after an absence of
over fifty years. Although the breeding-site of the ospreys was in a remote area of the Highlands, it seems probable that something like a
quarter of a million people will have visited the special observation hide
in the first ten years, always provided that the birds continue to return
to nest in the next three. Bird reservations in many countries tell much
the same story of a growing public interest in spending at least a day in
wild places watching wild creatures. Most people with knowledge consider that the only real hope for wild life in the developing countries of
Africa and Asia lies in their commercial value as a tourist-attraction.
There is little room left for idealism in the preservation of rare wild life

today. It is going to be difficult enough to save it all, anyway. Commercial exploitation, provided that it is in the best interests of conservation, is the most potent weapon in the locker.

What else have we got? How about the balance of nature? Usually one only has to mention this phrase to find oneself in a hornets' nest. The whole concept of the so-called balance of nature is so theoretical and our knowledge of the complex inter-relationships of plant and animal communities (all of which are affected by other complicated things such as soil and climate) is so rudimentary that this grand old war-horse, if not exactly a non-starter, seldom runs far in any reasonable argument. It is, after all, something of an academic exercise to remove mankind from any discussion of this kind. The principle behind the so-called balance is that control is ultimately exercised through the natural order of things. How far men can go, headlong and largely disregarding all but the immediate consequences, remains to be seen. That in his wisdom he can plumb the depths of folly is testified by the waste and the misery and the suffering of two world wars in the same half-century from both of which, collectively, he emerged with a colossal overdraft. But his stupidity can be demonstrated in many smaller ways. In Britain for the last thirty years a small fortune has been spent in trying to get almost every drop of rain-water back into the sea as quickly as possible. So the land has been parched and with the demand for water rapidly and steadily rising – not least for irrigation, much of which would otherwise not have been required – it is now becoming necessary to flood considerable areas of good agricultural land in order to create reservoirs to supply more water. There is no evidence that the brain-power and capital expenditure involved in the crusade for better drainage has been prudently invested – on the contrary. Nor is there much evidence that scientists and technologists are endowed with any more vision than the rest of us or that they are any less susceptible to the profit motive than you or I.

Whatever blame may ultimately be laid upon us and our fathers, it is only within the last hundred years that there has been any serious awakening to the threat to the wild life of the world. This process has quickened greatly during the present century (partly as a result of the obviously growing dangers) and in many countries today there are organisations whose energies are devoted to tackling the diverse problems of wild life management. The drawback is that in some countries there is an enormous amount of overlapping. In Great Britain, apart from the amenity bodies, anybody interested in the general preservation of wild life could, provided that he had the money, worthily subscribe to the World Wildlife Fund, the Fauna Preservation Society, the Council for Nature, the Wildfowl Trust, the Wildfowlers' Association of Great Britain and Ireland, the Royal Society for the Protection of Birds, the Game Research Association, the British Section of the International Council for Bird Preservation, the British Trust for Ornithology, the Mammal Society and the British Deer Society – even this does not exhaust the list. He will also be begged to support his local county Naturalists' Trust and he must also bear in mind the indirect benefit to wild life given by institutions like the National Trust and the Council for the Preservation of Rural England. A tiny fraction of his taxes will also be channelled off to support the Nature Conservancy – a state body founded in 1949 which has done superlative work on utterly inadequate funds. Few governments have been meaner in their support for nature-conservation than the British, of whatever political faction. The Dutch and the Americans have done much better. It is an extreme anachronism that, in Britain, not even a percentage of the very considerable revenue from gun and game licences is used to promote the game and fowl which makes the purchase of a licence worthwhile.

Even if the governments of some countries show less irresponsibility towards the preservation of wild life than others, it seems pretty certain that the main burden will fall on bodies like the World Wildlife Fund (which has been surprisingly ill-supported in the U S A.), the National Audubon Society, the Royal Society for the Protection of Birds and the Wildfowl Trust. But if the situation is urgent (and in many ways it is) it is lamentable that there should continue to be much overlapping, with the inevitable waste of vital funds on administration. In Great Britain there never was a more opportune moment for those with courage and vision to move boldly towards co-ordinating all the various wild life interests into one comprehensive body which would make itself responsible for wild life management and conservation within the United Kingdom, whilst at the same time making its proper contribution to conservation on a world basis. In my opinion British bird-protectionists should be abjectly ashamed at the miserable financial support which has been given to the British Section of the International Council for Bird Preservation. Granted that the machinery of this body is somewhat autocratic, to say the least, with a consequent lack of appeal to the ordinary member of the public who, rightly regarding himself as a shareholder, considers he ought to have some right, at least once a year, to have his say if he wants to. But this does not excuse the fact that the income of the British Section has been almost microscopic, whilst sister national organisations have been amassing enormous reserves.

Great Britain is not unique in this respect. But it is certainly a country in which birds and animals have suffered and in which they will continue to do so unless a more practical and broad-minded approach is made to the problems of conservation – problems which most of us know are urgent without having to be simultaneously told so by anything up to half a dozen bodies with near-identical objects. But it may help us to get a more balanced view of the situation if we see how the whole concept of conservation has developed in Great Britian, since the first laws designed solely for the protection of birds were made (and broken) almost 100 years ago.

2 The Historical Background

How did bird-protection come to be an organised force? It is, in fact, extremely difficult to answer what must sound a simple question. In Great Britain it is almost exactly 100 years since the first legislation was passed solely for the purpose of giving protection to birds other than for their preservation for sport. This law gave limited protection to the eggs of certain sea-birds. It is doubtful whether it made any significant difference to them, one way or the other. Eleven years later, in 1880, an Act was passed which was much wider in its scope geographically but which still only gave legal protection to a limited number of species and then only in the close season. Again there is no reason to suppose that this original Act of 1880 was of any practical value in itself. The protection was too limited and probably also too difficult to enforce. Yet it is of interest because it shows that, for one reason or another, some people were beginning to realise that wild birds were worth conserving – or, at least, some of them.

This book is not a treatise on English social life but if we are to follow in some detail the past history of bird-protection, it is important to bear in mind a number of points. The first one is the enormous value placed upon ownership and private property. Probably this was even more marked in the Victorian era than it is today, yet at the present time a man may be fined up to £100 or even sent to prison for a considerable period for poaching one or two salmon of which there are millions in British waters, whereas if he destroys an osprey, of which there are only two or three pairs in the whole country, he may be fined £25. The second point is that British governments have shown astonishingly little real interest in almost all matters connected with the countryside and the conservation of wild life. (Many countries – the USA, for instance – have been much better served in this respect.) The third point is that the public approach to bird-protection (and to the welfare of wild animals as a whole) has usually been largely emotional and often based upon complete ignorance of the facts.

The British Protection of Birds Act, 1880, gave no protection whatsoever to birds of prey, though a number of species were in dire need of practical help. The ospreys in the Scottish highlands, harried by St John and others, were approaching the end of their tether. One or two individual landowners did take some steps to safeguard the very few remaining pairs but the results were too local, too ineffective, to preserve the species and, as a consequence, this magnificent bird did not breed in Britain for over fifty years. It would be impossible now to say definitely that really effective legislation *would* have saved the osprey from being driven out of Britain but this hardly removes the guilt from any responsible government which failed to make the attempt.

Yet the outlook of the public – even the nature-loving public – was so different then from what it is today. Most sporting landowners would almost certainly have been opposed to any protection for birds of prey in 1880 because they were considered to do damage to game (and some species almost certainly did). But even those with a more sentimental approach often objected to the hawks and owls, seeing them as relentless killers of the little song birds they loved so much. Nor is this emotional view by any means dead. During my long period of service with the RSPB I had more than one letter directed against the cuckoo, which is cruel enough to lay its eggs in the nests of dear little birds like the robin, hedge sparrow and pied wagtail.

If the Act of 1880 was too weak in essence and largely ineffective in practice, it was at least what the historians might call a milestone in that it established the principle (if not, alas, the practice) that wild life, just because it was not privately owned, was not something which could always be destroyed by any member of the public who was so minded. In the nineteenth century there was a much greater commercial

interest in wild birds than there is today. Two things must be remembered, however, before one condemns such practices out of hand.
Firstly, to take a controlled crop of many wild creatures does not necessarily mean that they will become any less numerous. The potential rate
of increase of the majority of birds is so great that the main causes of
death are probably due to starvation, either directly or indirectly,
through such processes as weakly birds becoming more susceptible to
predators or through malnutrition leading to disease. Secondly, commercial interests, properly conducted, need not necessarily run counter
to the interests of conservation. These points can be pursued further in
due course and I will only mention here two which happen to be of
considerable topical interest.

For some twenty-five years prior to 1954 the eggs of the lapwing were
protected in Britain. Prior to that there had been a considerable, though
probably diminishing trade in the eggs which, even if some people consider them overrated, are certainly palatable. In 1954 it was argued,
on the one hand, that the lapwing population had been steadily declining in most areas and that their eggs should therefore continue to be
fully protected. The patent weakness in this case was the fact that a long
period of complete protection had failed to result in the species even
holding its own, let alone increasing. As legal shooting and netting had
also been virtually stopped by law, it seemed fairly obvious that other
factors were responsible for any decline in numbers. The possibility of
the protection of the eggs being of some benefit to the species, however,
could not be entirely ruled out, for without this help the decline *might*
have been more marked. A compromise was finally adopted whereby
lapwings' eggs could be legally taken up to, but not after, April 14th.
Arguments in favour were that almost all the birds which had their
clutches legally taken would lay again (a reasonable assumption) and
that in any event the early clutches were less likely to be successful, a
view which was countered by a statement that lapwings knew better
than Members of Parliament when to lay their eggs (and having had to
listen to all the debates on the 1954 Bill, I would rate that as highly
likely). Yet, even if we discount the anthropomorphic approach, it is
not sound to suggest that a bird knows best when to lay its eggs. In

many species there is often quite a long period, frequently several weeks in length, between the time when the first females lay and the last ones do so, while there is usually a comparatively short period during which the majority of the birds go down on eggs. If we accept the general principles of Natural Selection, it must be those birds which lay at or around the peak period who succeed in producing most off-spring. Clearly one cannot assist those birds which lay late by taking their eggs, for then, even if they lay again, it will be at a time still further removed from the optimum date. But if we take those eggs which are laid before the peak we should then only be making the hens lay again at a time when, on all the evidence available, they would have the best chances of ultimate success.

In the Netherlands there has probably always been a much greater commercial trade in lapwings' eggs than in Britain – at any rate in the present century. Most of this traffic is carried on in the province of Friesland, where it is legal to take the eggs until April 19th. Mr Ko Zweeres, the Secretary of the Dutch Bird Protection Society (*Neder-landse Vereeniging tot Bescherming van Vogels*) assured me recently that he had no reason to suppose that the taking of the eggs up to that date had had any adverse effect upon the numbers of the birds; he believed that the reverse might well be the case. The local farmers make a useful income from the sale of the early clutches. Being understandably anxious to ensure that this income is maintained in future years, they go to considerable trouble after the closing date to make certain that the nests are not disturbed and not needlessly destroyed by farming operations.

It would be a *non sequitur* to suggest that what is best in one area is also going to be best in another, but if, as is now proposed, the taking of lapwings' eggs at any time is to be banned by law, I hope that nobody will be misled into believing that this is likely to have any significant impact on the British population of lapwings.

If I have strayed from the main theme of this chapter, my object in discussing the lapwing and recent legislation was to show that, in spite of the fact that we now have much more ornithological knowledge (though not nearly enough) than did the pioneers in bird-protection in the latter half of the last century, we do not always bring it to bear with the necessary acumen and sense of scientific integrity and responsibility. Even now we are often as prone as ever (and the present writer is not immune from such criticism) to relapse into propaganda. The noble Lord who recently introduced the legislation which would give full protection to lapwings' eggs claimed that lapwings were beneficial to the farmer. Is this view really defensible? Is there any worthwhile evidence to suggest that the lapwing is any more helpful in modern husbandry than that the increasing number of gannets are detrimental to sea-fisheries? Is not the lapwing an attractive creature in its own right? Is there any better argument for trying to find out the actual facts behind the decline and to take practical, rather than theoretical, steps to endeavour to maintain our population in reasonable numbers?

It is easy now to see that in 1880 a good many wrong conclusions were drawn from insufficient evidence. There is no reason to suppose that, in 2050, our great-grandsons will not be able to say much the same about our own generation. Certainly eighty-five years ago the threats to some of our birds were different and perhaps sometimes much less clear-cut than they are now. It is not difficult to understand why the sportsman and his gamekeepers destroyed, if they could, any bird of prey or owl on sight. They took game and, in days when shooting was more competitive than it is now, success as often as not being rated by the size of the bag rather than the actual sport involved, anything which might have been considered to interfere with that end was dispatched if possible and by any means, fair or foul. It is doubtful, however, whether any of these sportsmen foresaw that some birds of prey would be brought to such a low level that they would be completely or virtually exterminated. Nor is there any certain evidence that they need have been. What is probable is that if the pressure from sportsmen had been exercised with a little discretion, some birds of prey might never have been brought so low. But did anybody have the knowledge upon which any prudent policy could be based? What is almost a certainty is that, had anybody attempted to secure adequate protection for birds of prey under the Protection of Birds Act of 1880, the Bill would never have had the remotest hope of reaching the statute book. What is even more pertinent is that even had such legislation been passed, it would not have had the slightest effect. Most landowners were a law unto themselves, even if a good many of them, as Justices of the Peace or Sheriffs, cheerfully dealt out justice to all and sundry in the name of the Queen.

Birds of prey, after all, were by no means the only British birds in a serious plight in the 1880's. The bittern, that curiously plumaged heron whose hollow, repetitive booming call is an integral part of any extensive reed marsh in spring, was on its last legs. The avocet had ceased to breed forty years earlier. The ruff and the black-tailed godwit had gone the same way. The sheldduck, believe it or not, was becoming a rarity save in a very few favoured localities. It would not be profitable to try to pursue the reasons for the ill-fortunes which attended many species. We can guess at some of the factors involved. But animal populations are apt to fluctuate in ways which often defy explanation. Mr James Fisher and Mr Roger Tory Peterson, in *The World of Birds*, quote an estimate of the population of the passenger pigeon of America at its peak as between three and five billion and add that in the thirty years, 1866–1896, the estimated annual slaughter averaged 1,200,000. An annual cull of less than one per cent cannot, by itself, have accounted for the extinction of the species. The wryneck, in Britain, has declined to the point of near-extinction without suffering any obvious persecution by man. On the other hand, the collared dove has exploded from Asia right across Europe with a rapidity and strength which is inexplicable and the fulmar – a rather noxious bird with magnificent powers of flight – has recently spread almost all round the coasts of Britain, though less than 100 years ago it was, we think, confined to St Kilda in the Outer Hebrides, where it formed one of the principal sources of food for the islanders until the evacuation in 1930.

In the early days of protection, sentiment was the motivating force. Towards the end of the nineteenth century there was a flourishing traffic in caged birds. This was partly due to the fact that in Britain at that time there was a good deal of real poverty. A poor man in what spare time he had or if he was out of work could set his nets and spread his bird-lime and capture enough victims to buy a good many loaves of bread. But any trade demands buyers as well as sellers and buyers of pretty things in cages have never been found wanting. Whether it is ethical for man to capture creatures and force upon them an unnatural life in captivity until they die is largely a matter for individual conscience and not a subject which can be dealt with in detail here. On the one hand it can be argued that, say, a bullfinch in a cage is freed from the risk of starvation in cold weather or sudden death at the claws of some predator. Birds in the wild, if they are happy at all (and we cannot prove that point, either way), are probably quite untroubled by thoughts of death and food shortage. But the campaign to prevent the caging of wild birds in Britain has been waged ever since 1880 with very reasonable success. The law is still widely broken, though the RSPCA and the RSPB succeed from time to time in bringing offenders to book and courts are tending to impose penalties salutary enough to act as a deterrent. Most of these cases are good propaganda but they matter little in the field of real conservation. The height of folly has, in fact, been reached in the case of the beautiful bullfinch, which, in much of England, it is legal to kill but which cannot be sold to those who might like to keep an amenable small bird in a cage. So bullfinches trapped by the fruitgrower have their necks wrung, which some may feel is an ironical comment on modern bird-protection.

Eschewing the ethical pros and cons, there seems little doubt that, on conservational grounds alone, a limited number of certain small birds could be taken from the wild each autumn without any diminution in the overall stocks. It is still perfectly legal in Britain to buy and keep exotic birds, though in these cases there is not only a much greater risk of death and hardship in transit but often a strong probability that the catching is carried out with the minimum of humanity.

Whilst the traffic in cage birds was one of the main preoccupations of the earlier protectionists, it was the plumage trade which gave birth to the Royal Society for the Protection of Birds, one of the oldest and most vigorous bird protection societies in the world. In 1889, in Croydon (not then a County Borough but a small town in the county of Surrey) a small group of humanitarian women met together and decided to form what they called the Fur, Fin and Feather group. The ladies were indeed pioneers in a rough and hostile world. We cannot assess accurately the debt which we owe to them, but it is pretty considerable. What one does wonder is just what the menfolk were doing. The British Ornithologists' Union had then been in existence for over thirty years. Its members, as well as those of other learned bodies like the Zoological Society of London (founded in 1829) ought to have been much more aware of the need for conservation of wild life. No doubt some of these more scientific minds were not wholly ignorant on the matter: Professor Alfred Newton had been one of the driving forces behind the first bird-protection Act of 1869. The fact remains that it was left to a group of sentimentalists to take any concerted action.

There was something of tragedy in this, however, in that these early pioneers appear often to have been ignorant about ornithological matters. Those with the necessary knowledge, who could so easily have been of enormous benefit to the protection movement in its earliest days, stood aloof – not only stood aloof but were apparently ready to criticise those errors which could have been avoided with their support.

The Fur, Fin and Feather group was short-lived. Within a year it had become the Society for the Protection of Birds, with a small headquarters in London. Its first objective was to draw attention to the iniquities involved in the flourishing trade in so-called 'osprey' plumes. At that time it was the fashion of aristocratic ladies to bedeck themselves with these feathers (and very beautiful they were) which came from adult egrets. The 'osprey' plumes were only developed by egrets in the breeding season. The birds were destroyed in their nesting colonies in Spain and elsewhere simply for the few feathers which, because women wanted to wear them, fetched relatively high prices, not only in Britain but in many other European countries. The slaughter was colossal and, at least in some cases, the adults were killed when they had young in the nest, the latter being left to die miserably – though not, let us remember, any more miserably than a brood of small nestlings whose dam may have been killed by a passing automobile.

The crusade against the plumage trade gathered momentum. Many women, and some men, were profoundly shocked by the illustrated leaflets produced by the Society. Some of the women, in all probability, arrived at meetings clad in expensive fur coats, the production of which may well have caused suffering to animals beside which the pain of the luckless egrets was insignificant. This, perhaps, was one reason why it was a pity that the Society abandoned its original title of Fur, Fin and Feather. Another and stronger reason for regretting the change was that until very recently the approach to conservation in Britain was a singularly narrow one, almost wholly confined to birds. Even now, in the middle of the 1960's, it is astonishing that little or no protection is given to most other wild animals, though a good many are in much greater need of care and protection than most birds.

America did not suffer in quite the same way. The Audubon Societies usually took a much wider view of their responsibilities. When the National Audubon Society was founded in 1905 it covered all aspects of natural life, though it is true that birds have always been its primary concern. It is a pity that the protection movement in Britain has not so far developed along much broader lines. Although there are now signs of change, it is not only late in the day but the trend is towards disintegration, with all its risks of overlapping, divided strength and heavy administrative costs, instead of towards a unified policy of wild life management which is what the situation demands.

It took the Society for the Protection of Birds over thirty years before it succeeded in moving the British Government to pass legislation banning the import of 'osprey' plumes. By that time the Society had grown apace and broadened its activities. In 1904 it had received signal recognition by incorporation under Royal Charter and so became the Royal Society for the Protection of Birds. Many leading figures were connected with it, notably Sir Edward Grey – later Lord Grey of Falloden – and W. H. Hudson, who for many years enjoyed a great reputation both in Britain and the United States and who, in spite of his patent shortcomings and his present undeserved eclipse, probably did more to influence public opinion in favour of wild life than any other writer of the present century. Hudson was, with respect, an ornithologist who had gone to seed. Born in the Argentine in 1840 and reared in the broad spaces of the pampas, the latter part of his life, spent in England, seemed to have had a profound and melancholy effect upon him. But his avowed policy (not invariably practised) 'to pet nothing and persecute nothing' at least enabled him to avoid much of the sickly sentiment of the Edwardian era. At that time, too, the young Society was attracting a number of good ornithologists, such as the late E. G. B. Meade-Waldo and P. W. Munn. It was beginning to set up bird sanctuaries and to employ wardens during the breeding season in remote areas like the Shetland Islands.

It never ceased to agitate for amendments to the law, which was largely a dead letter. Egg-collectors had become a real menace to rare species. The red kite, once a common bird of prey, had dwindled by 1905 to a remnant of five or six pairs, all confined to an area of central Wales. This decline was not caused by oologists, any more than the decline of the osprey and other species, but once the critical stage had been reached they could have destroyed our British kites for ever. What is more to the point is that they would have done so if they could, just as they may have done (for if they failed it was not for want of trying) in the case of the osprey.

If egg-collectors are not indigenous to Britain, they have only reached plague proportions in that country, though many have collected eggs from abroad. Although they must have vexed the RSPB in its early years much more than they do today, they are still with us and must be given some space in any discussion on bird conservation. If a lot of nonsense has been talked by egg-collectors, a good deal has also been talked by those who are opposed to their activities. In the first place, to collect the eggs of various species for scientific purposes is neither more nor less venal than to collect specimens. Fanatics of the type who shout that every creature is entitled to its own life might voice their objections even to museum collections, though how they think all the information that is in the bird handbooks would otherwise have been provided is anybody's guess. Scientific collections, whether of skins or eggs, are one thing. Uncontrolled or indiscriminate collecting is another. Even reputable museums are suspect in this connection, particularly some of those in the USA. If a stuffed specimen or a skin of a bird or animal in a museum is invaluable, nobody – least of all a responsible museum director – should ever for one moment forget that the living creature is priceless. No museum has the remotest right to encourage even in the slightest degree, either directly or indirectly, the killing of any rare species. Subject to this proviso, the collection of specimens for important national institutions (in which I am even prepared to include the Natural History Museum in London) must surely be not only permissible but much to be encouraged provided they are in a position to make proper use of them, especially by making them readily available for serious students.

Egg-collections may well be less valuable than skin-collections but this is a relative point. The rather sharp gibe sometimes levelled at egg-collectors that an egg-shell is nothing more than a pigmented fragment of calcium carbonate is just about on a par with saying that an Old Master is nothing more than coloured substances smeared on a strip of cheap canvas. Apart from the fact that many bird's eggs are aesthetically pleasing to any but the most jaundiced eye, a great deal *has* been learnt by some of those who have collected them. For instance, the activities of men like E. C. Stuart Baker and Edgar Chance in connection with cuckoos' eggs, did teach us all a great deal and certainly did no apparent damage to the species concerned. It is also important to realise that the serious type of egg-collector was not only a good ornithologist (if he had not been he would not have found many eggs) but often did a great deal of watching as well as collecting. The protectionists in their arguments against collectors (and in some other matters too) have not infrequently seriously weakened their case and damaged their own integrity by bringing charges against egg-collectors which – unless they were singularly stupid – they must have known were wholly or partly false.

But if the opponents of egg-collectors have been extravagant in their language, they can scarcely have excelled some of the propaganda trotted out by the oologists. I can only summarise these in the most general terms, but they run like this. 'Egg-collecting has never been responsible for the extinction of any birds.' In 1958 an unknown individual, displaying skill, courage and considerable knowledge, raided the nest of the only pair of ospreys breeding in Britain in that summer. Apart from that glaring and recent example, there is plenty of evidence, admittedly sometimes circumstantial, to show that species on the edge

Protecting birds from the bird-watcher.
Bert Axell, the warden at Minsmere, Suffolk,
conducting visitors out of the famous
tree hide.

Each summer 20,000 people follow this
signpost to the nesting-site of the ospreys
at Loch Garten, Scotland.

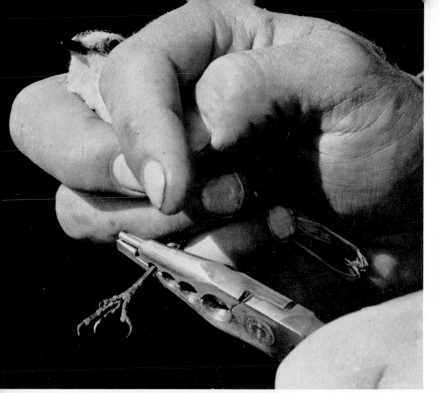

Much knowledge has been gained by competent ringing: many birds have been killed or injured through the impatience or inexperience of pseudo-scientists.

Millions of birds have been needlessly killed by deliberate pumping of foul oil into the seas. The victims here are razorbill, guillemot and red-throated diver.

of extinction have undoubtedly been plundered. The red kite and the marsh harrier are two specific examples. 'Only first clutches are taken by responsible collectors. The bird then always lays a repeat clutch.' The second part of this statement is not true of all species and any person who makes a statement of this kind is either abysmally ignorant or mendacious. The idea that only first clutches are taken is nonsense. If a person finds a clutch of eggs, how can he always be certain that it is not a 'repeat'? However, quite apart from this, there is again evidence to show that collectors have taken clutch after clutch. Not many years ago, when I was involved in the unpleasant task of assisting the police whilst they were executing a search-warrant in the house of a man who was subsequently convicted of aiding and abetting a dealer in eggs, his own data cards showed that he had collected, during a single summer, five clutches laid by a particular hen of a pair of rare Dartford warblers and on the back of one card was a note recording the fact that, though he had marked down the nest, some other wretch had been infamous enough to forestall him, thus preventing his personal triumph of securing every egg laid by the unfortunate bird during the whole of one season.

It may be difficult for some people to realise that, at one time, the main argument advanced against any type of egg-collecting was the cruelty caused to the broody bird. Indeed, there are still many people interested in but largely ignorant of the subject, who believe this to be true. But birds behave in an essentially practical way. Most species lose far too high a proportion of their eggs and young from purely natural causes, to have either the time or the instinct to go into mourning. A passerine bird which loses her brood of well-grown nestlings to a marauding corvid in the morning may well be busily building a new nest by evening, in readiness for a further clutch of eggs which she will probably start laying within a week.

Soon after it was formed the RSPB began to turn its attention to schoolchildren. This led, in 1904, to the famous Bird and Tree Scheme which flourished for many years in schools – admittedly only a fractional percentage at best – throughout the country. One beauty of this scheme was its simplicity. A school enrolled pupils as 'cadets' at a nominal sum of one penny each. Each pupil had to choose a particular bird or tree, watch it for a season and then write an essay covering his or her observations. The ages of the competitors varied between 6 or 7 and 14. Some of the entries were unconsciously very funny. There is a basis of good fact and a singular vividness in the essay of a girl who wrote: 'Periodically there are plagues of voles and field mice, and at this time the owls are drawn by telegraphy to the spots where they are. This causes them to lay larger eggs at a rapid rate.' Another girl, writing about the chaffinch, might not have been such a good observer, but at least she realised that the concept of feathered friends depended upon one's point of view. 'I saw a chaffinch tapping the ground with its beak. I had been told they did this to make the worm come up thinking it was raining. I think this is a very cunning way of getting food but it isn't fair to worms.' Some were rather more fiction than fact. One year when I was judge of the Wiltshire essays (the competition worked on a county basis, with handsome prize-shields for the winning school) a charming young lady of eight chose to watch a pair of house martins which were about to breed in a previous year's nest under the eaves just outside her bedroom window. In a commendably brief essay it was recorded that the bird laid her eggs on Friday, that they hatched out on the following morning and that the parent birds were busy all that day catching and bringing flies to their lovely babies, whilst on the Sunday the young martins safely left the nest.

Although it was never intended to do so, it is difficult to believe that this operation did not encourage a good many country children to hunt for nests and, more often than not, to take eggs. Having lived in various small villages almost all my life I am satisfied that egg-collecting by village boys is not a thing to be discouraged. The ignorance of many countrymen about wild animals which do not immediately impinge on their lives is almost as incredible as that of the average country-loving townsman who sallies into the fields and who can identify a bee-orchid or a yellow wagtail but who has no idea whether a field is growing *brassicae* or sugar-beet, what the difference is between a Friesian or a Hereford cow nor perhaps even (to the benefit of the far-mer!) the difference between a bullock and a bull. Many village boys still know nothing of the law. They still enjoy the thrill and skill of hunting with a catapult (one of the most humane weapons in the armoury) just as they still enjoy hunting for nests in the early spring.

Granted that activities of this kind cannot be said to be directed towards conservational ends. It is, however, equally important to realise that the damage done to conservation, even assuming it exists at all, is negligible. What is pertinent is that boys who indulge in these activities acquire a broad knowledge of, and an interest in, wild life. They may not, like some of the higher-powered and more academically-minded young naturalists, spend their adult leisure poking and prying into the private lives of this or that creature, but they will probably remain stubborn allies of any movement to preserve the natural order of things. At the risk of sticking my neck out I would suggest that undesirable and destructive nest-ragging, which is becoming more prevalent, and certainly does more harm than the village egg-collectors ever did, has been indirectly fostered by the atmosphere of taboo which has fallen upon the young country hunter. In suppressing something which really does not matter overmuch, one way or the other, we may have encouraged something purely destructive to take its place.

Bird-nesting boys tend to find nests most often either early in the season, before the foliage sprouts, or those which are most conspicuously placed. These are the very nests which are either most likely to fail in a spell of inclement weather or – and perhaps this is a more important point – they will probably be discovered and plundered by some predator. It could be argued that the taking of the eggs from these early and conspicuous nests might actually help the birds concerned to rear more young in a season. Those which might otherwise lose their nestlings to predators will have lost, alas, two or three valuable weeks of the breeding season. The young ornithologist, serious enough to study just what happens to a clutch of eggs, painstakingly noting how many are laid and on what dates, how long the eggs take to hatch and how many do so, and how many young finally fledge, may well bring disaster to a bird whose nest was otherwise well hidden by leaving tell-tale tracks or opening up the surroundings of the nest. It is not beyond the wit and curiosity of a watching crow or magpie to fly down on the departure of the ornithologist to discover just what the disturbance was all about. Good intentions and practical conservation are not necessarily good bedmates. Conservational issues are seldom anything like as clear-cut as some of the 'diehard' protectionists would have us believe.

Organisations like the RSPB and the Audubon Societies in North America have always regarded education as of considerable importance. Only the most myopic would cavil at this, whether it be at a juvenile or an adult level. But education, whilst it should be aesthetic as well as factual, should never be relegated to a form of mass-propaganda. It is a fact that the golden eagle is a relatively rare bird in Britain: it is a fact that it is one of the largest birds of prey; it is a fact that eagles are illegally shot and their eggs illegally plundered by collectors; it is a fact that there is strong circumstantial evidence that residues of toxic substances used in sheep-dips are affecting their fertility and could, if not checked, have extremely adverse effects, perhaps imperilling the very existence of the species. It is not a fact that a golden eagle soaring high over a highland glen is a marvellous and uplifting sight: it is a feeling unlikely to be shared by a shepherd who believes, rightly or wrongly, that eagles have been taking some of his new-born lambs. The same principle must apply with the songs of the European blackbird and the nightingale. Both are well-developed songs, both are musical by Western standards, but whether you prefer the one to the other is not an objective matter of fact but of subjective feeling. The scratchy outbursts of the whitethroat appear to serve its natural purpose just as effectively as the louder, longer coloratura outpourings of the nightingale. If man does not live by bread alone, he is wise to be practical when it comes to the pinch. Face to face with an angry leopard even the most ardent conservationist would be unlikely to put beauty before ballistics. I doubt if it is entirely fortuitous that the conservation movement is most highly-developed in those countries of the world in which wild life dangerous to man has either been exterminated or else brought under strict control. The British people, with a very few exceptions, are still very fearful of adders and happily kill grass snakes in their efforts to be rid of them.

This simple matter of the viper and the grass snake is one way in which we can best appreciate the weakness of education. We cannot, apparently, expect an educational system to turn out children who can use a compass, read a one-inch ordnance map or grasp the essentials of natural history as distinct from basic biology. At the very moment of writing this my wife has brought me a fledgling which has tumbled out of a sparrow's nest. What effort do we make to ensure that children can humanely dispatch small animals in trouble? Perhaps nowhere better than in our treatment of sick and wounded creatures can we best see how easy it is for emotions to murder our moral obligations.

The Zoological Society of London is an old and august institution. It is supported by zoologists of repute and produces scientific publications in keeping with its reputation. Yet it also produces the chimpanzees' tea-party. I am not suggesting that the chimps do not enjoy the whole performance; I would dare to suggest that this is not a good way of getting young people to appreciate wild life. The difficulty, of course, is to try to find what is the best way. It is a problem made all the more difficult in most countries because most children are reared in urban areas. St James's Park may be one of the finest places in Britain to look at duck, but it is somewhat artificial, conveying the impression that the natural order of things is a bed of roses for all concerned, with all found and some exotic pelicans thrown in for good measure. Even when the town child is taken into the country, much of the time may be spent whizzing along in a box on wheels.

The concept of Nature Trails (a title which may well strike a young and eager mind as just about as deadly as the positively dreadful Nature Study) was started in the United States and is in the process of being developed in Britain. Whether it will spread to more logically-minded countries remains to be seen. An open air sign-posted track through a nature reserve has much to commend it, no doubt. It enables one to control – in theory at least – a considerable number of people. This is, to some extent, a negative virtue, for it would be better for the wild life if they were not there at all. On the other hand we cannot hope to get adequate support for conserving wild life, financial or otherwise, unless we can let people enjoy it so far as is possible and so come to realise its value.

There is a close parallel between Nature Trails and the control of people in bird reserves and wild life parks. I do not propose to treat of reserves and refuges in detail until later, but they fit into the historical theme which is at the back of this chapter. The RSPB first started to think in terms of bird reserves around the turn of the century but there were in fact private reserves in existence before that time, even if they were not given such a title and little or nothing was known of them. A hundred years ago the great skua or bonxie, a species with a restricted range in the North Atlantic, had declined to the edge of extinction in Britain, holding on only in very small numbers in two islands in the Shetland group, the isolated island of Foula and on the great promontory of Hermaness on the island of Unst, the northernmost land in Britain. The suggestion that the decline in the fortunes of the great skua was due to egg-collectors is untenable. Skuas were not popular with the local crofters in the nineteenth century any more than they are today. Had it not been for the Edmundsson family, owners of Hermaness, the great skua might have followed in the wake of the avocet, ruff, black-tailed godwit, bittern and marsh harrier and ceased to breed if only, like some of these others, for a limited period.

The Edmundsson's gave special protection to the few remaining pairs and before the First World War the RSPB paid a tiny gratuity to a local man to act as a part-time warden in the nesting season. The result has been an astonishing increase in the numbers of skuas, though once the critical minimum had been passed, there is no particular credit due to the earlier, and probably vital, conservation measures. In fact the species has since spread in some strength into the Orkneys, some of the Hebridean islands and onto the Scottish mainland.

The idea of using local men to work as part-time wardens in the breeding season was extended by the RSPB as resources permitted. Simple as it may seem today, it was a satisfactory arrangement, not only giving excellent value for money, but engendering a great deal of local goodwill. The Society also began to acquire reserves, though they called them sanctuaries. As time went by they came in for a good deal of criticism on the grounds that they failed to check crows and other predators. This charge may not have been unfounded, though one suspects that it was exaggerated. For many years the Society was at logger-heads, not unnaturally, with the egg-collectors, who used any stick, true or false, to beat what was all too often and wrongly described as a Society of old ladies. One of these 'old ladies', who got no medals and whose name, Linda Gardiner, has been almost forgotten was for a long period around the time of the First World War and after the only full-time salaried person on the staff of the RSPB. Yet in 1922, after many years of service, she got a wage increase which brought her emoluments to £2 10s. a week. Even allowing for the depreciation in the value of money this illustrates the point that those who devoted their energies to bird protection were dedicated people not in it for the money. The fact of the matter is that an organisation like the RSPB forty or fifty years ago simply could not afford to pay any more. It worked on a shoe-string with an income of the order of about one per cent of what it controls today.

Between the two World Wars conservation in Britain tended to run out of steam. The division between those people who would have re-garded themselves as ornithologists and those who were concerned with conservation was still very wide. Nor is it easy at this distance of time fully to understand why this was so. Probably the protectionists were still too sentimental and unrealistic in their approach to many prob-lems and perhaps they were unduly suspicious of anything that smacked of the scientific. They were always, of course, under pressure from pub-lic opinion even as they still are today, and any form of egg-collecting or specimen hunting would probably have been regarded by the lay mem-ber to have been contrary to the principles of the Society for the Pro-tection of Birds, and it is even probable that, if any control of certain unwanted species in a bird sanctuary was carried out, it was undesirable to inform the membership. A personal anecdote may illustrate this point. When at the end of the Second World War I first joined the staff of the RSPB and with the minimum of essential qualifications was put in charge of bird reserves, it was considered at one of the meetings of the Watchers Committee that some control of magpies on one sanctuary was essential. But it was suggested that this should be done *sub rosa* as members would be unlikely to approve the procedure because they would not be able to appreciate the reasons behind it. I have not re-belled very often, but this suggestion seemed to me not only immoral but extremely pointless. In my own experience, if you will explain to people lucidly why it is essential to do something, a large majority will back your action. Indeed I would suggest that one of the reasons why protectionists have sometimes run into difficulties and alienated in-telligent public sympathy, not only in Great Britain but in other countries as well, has been due to the fact that they have funked the essential issue of telling the plain and unvarnished truth.

3 The Concept of the Bird Reserve

Although a bird reserve is, in a sense, a sanctuary for certain birds and although the term 'sanctuary' is still often used and has the older tradition, I think it will be better in this book to use the generally accepted name of bird reserve. I would add, however, that an even better name is a wild life reserve, for it is doubtful if we now have any right to devote any area entirely to the preservation of birds alone, even though they may often deserve priority.

The difficulties of running a bird reserve are enormous and will be dealt with later, but in following the evolution of reserves it is easy to see that the original concept was almost childishly simple. After purchasing or leasing an area, one put up barbed wire and notice boards, appointed a warden if one could afford one and then left it at that. Sometimes these reserves carried a stock of rare or uncommon birds, but as often as not they were small parcels of attractive woodland or some other relatively common habitat. Viewed from the narrow angle of necessary conservation, there was often nothing in them of any peculiar merit, and there is sometimes no reason to suppose that the bird life would have suffered in any way had no active steps been taken to purchase the land or acquire a lease; in some cases, quite the contrary. Public curiosity being what it is, the moment you designate, say, a small woodland as a bird sanctuary there will be a temptation for people to break into it.

Whether any damage will be done by such entry is beside the point, for one basic requirement of any wild life reserve must surely be to control unauthorised entry, which does not necessarily involve excluding all but the self-chosen few. There seems little doubt that in some of these early reserves there was a good deal of poaching of game, though seldom on any serious scale. The fundamental drawback arose from the idea, only recently exploded, that the great thing to do was to leave nature to her own devices.

As a general principle the main effort in a bird reserve must be directed to fighting natural processes. To allow certain birds such as crows and magpies to nest under ideal conditions may well result in the downfall of those very species which it is most desired to encourage. Equally it is almost invariably essential to manage the habitat so that it remains in the best possible condition. To allow an area of reedland to develop by an inevitable natural progression into Alder Carr is as good a way as any of getting rid of rare species like the marsh harrier, the bittern and the bearded tit. Equally, a woodland which may support an outstanding population of warblers, woodpeckers, tits and other birds will eventually reach maturity and relapse into a long decline. Such a change may well greatly benefit woodpeckers and other less adaptable woodland birds, but, unless some replanting is done, the whole character of the wood is bound to alter in time.

If we understand all this rather better now, it must be remembered that scientific conservation is a comparatively recent concept. Forty years ago the complex interdependence of flora and fauna, which today makes up the vital science of ecology, was virtually unknown. It still seems to me that the fundamental reason behind many of the early bird reserves or sanctuaries was to appeal to public opinion; to advertise a place where birds and especially small birds or sea-birds could nest allegedly at least in peace and security.

The importance of the rare bird does not appear to have been appreciated nearly so much thirty or forty years ago. Whilst no one can say with certainty, it seems likely that our so-called song-birds were just as common then – if not more so – than they are today. They were really in no need of any special protection whatsoever and it now seems a pity that more efforts were not made to help those species in greater need. It is odd, for instance, to consider the way in which the wryneck has declined during the present century without any serious efforts being made by conservationists to discover the reason why. To some extent, at least, this may be due to the fact that the general public have never heard of the wryneck, let alone seen it. It was the birds with which the public were familiar – the song thrush, blackbird, chaffinch and the garden titmice in fact, and the nightingale and other birds known through poetry, for which it was possible to arouse emotional sympathy. It may be difficult to understand it today, but half a century ago one suspects that golden eagles, bitterns and marsh harriers were not of much value in publicising protection.

Bird photographers have done some terrible things to rare wild life, but they have undoubtedly made a tremendous contribution to conservation in enabling the public to understand and appreciate creatures which they might otherwise never have seen at all.

Although, generally speaking, bird reserves in Britain between the two World Wars were relatively unimportant by modern standards, they were not beset by the problem of handling visitors. Apart from the fact that permits to visit were not available without some difficulty (and in some cases not available at all) there were almost certainly far fewer applicants in any case. The membership of the RSPB was a fraction of what it is today and in any event bird-watching had not developed into that fashionable semi-commercial pursuit which has simultaneously done so much both for the good and ill of birds. It seems likely that many other European countries were on the same footing – at least in those comparatively few where any serious conservation was practised. In the United States, on the other hand, the development of reserves proceeded along very different lines and with at least some help from the Federal and some State governments. For one thing the development of National Parks probably made it somewhat easier for the Audubon Societies to develop reserve programmes in some sort of alignment with those of the State and American efforts were undoubtedly helped by the fact that there was a somewhat closer understanding between sportsmen and protectionists than was the case in Britain. It was one of the saddest as well as one of the maddest major disasters in the history of bird protection in England that two groups of individuals with most of the essential things in common managed to indulge in the extravagant luxury of disputing matters of relatively little importance to either.

It is a little more difficult to understand why the State did so little in Britain in the field of conservation until after the Second World War. It would almost be fair to say that it did nothing at all. If the British people and most of their governments have always set considerable store by that part of their national heritage which consists of the countryside and all that goes with it, it does border upon the incredible that so much of it was allowed to be destroyed with little more than the odd genuflection from the planners and a great deal of oratory which echoes down the tunnel of history like so much tub-thumping. There is no doubt that opportunity after opportunity was lost by the general apathy which seems to be indigenous to British politicians as soon as they pay any attention to matters which are outside doctrinaire party politics. If a tenth of the effort which has been put into nationalising, denationalising and now perhaps renationalising the steel industry and nationalising and half-denationalising public transport – if one-tenth of the effort and money involved had been used in the development of National Parks which were really National Parks and not simply coloured areas on a map, we should have more of our national heritage to show today and more areas of real value to wild life.

When the British Trust for Ornithology was founded in 1933 it is a little ironical that most of its original endowment came from a great protectionist, Lord Grey, who had taken a considerable interest, often of a fanatical nature, in the affairs of the RSPB, yet broadly speaking the BTO and the RSPB were scarcely on speaking terms. The split here was undoubtedly between the extreme scientific outlook and the largely sentimental one. Outwardly there was a veneer of cordiality but the schism was there all the same. There is no point in trying to apportion any blame for a state of affairs which did little good to conservation. In any event, the BTO like the BOU appeared to be little concerned with the development of nature reserves. Ill-supported by modern standards and with little money, it was concerned mainly with the development of the so-called co-operative inquiry in which individual organisers worked on some problem in which many amateur ornithologists spread all over the country were able to assist; and the BTO was also concerned with the development of bird ringing or banding, which had been started before the First World War but which was there still in its infancy when judged by the position in the 1960's.

It seems likely that some of this scientific research, amateur or not, could have been channelled into some of the problems of conservation and perhaps especially reserve management, but one is bound to doubt whether the protectionists would have been very willing to accept any scientific advice, which many of them would have regarded as suspect on principle.

Before the War any shooting on a sanctuary was usually regarded as incompatible with its purpose. In principle there may be something to be said for this and indeed nowadays many sportsmen are only too well aware of the fact that without reserves they would soon go out of business themselves. The organised wildfowlers have for years been busily engaged with the Nature Conservancy and the Wildfowl Trust in designating many important areas as wildfowl refuges where no shooting takes place. The result has been an improvement in stocks and better sport for all, but it is singularly unlikely that it would have been possible to get such a view across in the 1930's. On one reserve in the south of England which was owned by the RSPB (but which they have since been sensible enough to sell) there was a large colony of gulls of no particular importance, but some breeding duck which were certainly worth protecting. Yet so great was the general hostility of sportsmen to the efforts of the Society at that time that the adjacent landowner made a point of erecting hides or blinds immediately outside the reserve and shooting at the duck at the earliest possible date which at that time was August 1st. As many of the locally reared duck on the reserve were then flappers, the decimation was considerable. This perhaps was an extreme case but it underlines the almost incredible lack of foresight displayed by most people who, for one reason or another, wanted to have birds but who were too blindly irresponsible to get together and do something about it.

Even at the time of the outbreak of the Second World War the RSPB had achieved relatively little in the promotion of worthwhile and properly managed bird reserves, but sneering is one of the least intelligent occupations and the fact that the Society had achieved as much as it had on slender resources and with relatively little help from ornithologists, is remarkable enough.

4 The Post-War Revolution

Some day somebody with sufficient time and knowledge may write a book upon the effects of major wars on wild life. No doubt the effects are partly good and partly bad, but certainly things occurred during Hitler's war in Europe which undoubtedly benefited wild birds. In England, for instance, the deliberate flooding of some coastal areas resurrected marshlands which had long been drained. In the Low Countries too there had been some flooding, though not all of it intentional. One result of some of these disturbances in the Netherlands may have given rise to the return to Britain of the avocet, a sensational post-war scoop which hit the headlines with a vengeance. It is an odd story.

The avocet had ceased to breed in Britain more than 100 years earlier. Its downfall has been variously attributed to drainage of the fens, the exploitation of its eggs for the making of pancakes and the collecting of birds for specimens. There were no doubt a lot of factors involved and we shall never now know the truth of it, but if a pair could return and breed successfully when the available habitat has been reduced much further, it certainly seems unlikely that the diminishing fens was a major factor in its departure. Indeed, had it been let alone it might have returned long ago, for during the 1860's there are a number of records of birds shot in the Thames estuary. We do not know now for certain when this striking black and white wader, with its delicate black upswept bill and elegant slate-blue legs, did first nest again, though there is a perfectly authentic record of two pairs breeding in Eire in 1938, though, like the exotic bee-eaters which bred in a Sussex sandpit in 1955 and the black-winged stilts on Nottingham sewage farm in 1947, the Irish avocets never returned. But there were several records of nesting birds during the War in coastal areas from the Wash to Essex. One clutch of eggs was almost certainly taken by a collector and another egg-collector who discovered a pair of avocets nesting in Essex in 1944 may or may not have been disappointed by the fact that they had small chicks when he found them.

I met up with the avocets in a rather astonishing way. I had been with the RSPB about a year and had got particularly interested in Suffolk because the Society was negotiating with the landowner for a lease of the famous marsh at Minsmere. This 300-acre marsh, which had been re-formed by salt water flooding in 1940, was still under requisition by the War Office. Actually at the time it extended to considerably more than 300 acres and a fight was brewing as to how much of it was likely to be saved from those responsible for pushing the claims of agriculture. But in fact I knew nothing, at the beginning of the warm, dry summer of 1947, of the fact that avocets had turned up at Minsmere and were being watched over by a team of local enthusiasts. The secret was well kept and I think rightly so. Sooner or later I should have discovered it and in any event the land had not yet been taken over by the RSPB. Save in exceptional circumstances it is almost invariably in the interests of nesting rare birds that their whereabouts should not be known, unless they are on reserves which can be adequately wardened. In making this statement I am not thinking only of the nefarious activities of unscrupulous egg-collectors, but also of irresponsible bird photographers (some of whom are highly competitive and always want to get in first) and of bird-watchers who are just as keen to record the rarity and who, in their keenness to try to record whether it is nesting or not, unwittingly (or, perhaps I should say, witlessly) ensure that it does not.

But to get back to my own part in the avocet story, one day early in July of 1947, I walked into the old RSPB offices in Victoria Street to be greeted by an agitated colleague with the story that a member of the council was on the telephone and was talking about some avocets

This oiled guillemot is almost certainly doomed to a long and painful death. Man, in his position as the most intelligent animal, need not and should not have allowed this sort of thing to happen.

A golden eagle shot when leaving her eyrie. The head was presumably removed as a trophy.

Most birds of prey are rapidly declining. These heads of wedge-tailed eagles reveal one of the reasons why.

which he had discovered breeding on an island in Suffolk. I have to admit to my shame that I regarded this as nonsense and promptly seized the telephone to find out what was really at stake. I learnt that on the previous day, which was a Sunday, my informant, Bob Hollis, had been taken by a friend down the river from Orford to an island called Havergate (which I had then never even heard of) and that he had seen three or four pairs of avocets which apparently had young. To say that I was excited would be a masterly understatement, yet I do not think that it would do any harm now to say that when this matter came to be discussed at a higher level, the general conclusion was that nothing could be done, that the birds would probably be all right any way and so on and so forth. Fresh from six years in the Air Force and perhaps unduly accustomed to action, and irritated (as indeed perhaps I have always been by talk of difficulties and disasters) I felt incredibly frustrated. However, it was agreed that if I wanted to I could go down and investigate. When I got to the little village of Orford I had to contact a local man who looked after the island for the then owner who lived in Yorkshire. I discovered that this chap was thinking of writing a letter to a popular daily newspaper to report the presence of the avocets or awl birds, as they were called locally. I went to the island that evening and discovered that the birds were breeding on a part which had been accidentally flooded with sea-water by a defective sluice, left by the army who had been in occupation during the War.

Nothing was said of this small colony of avocets on Havergate Island and it is amusing now to think that there were in fact two colonies only about twelve miles apart and that, although the guardians of each group did meet, no hint was dropped and it was some months before the full story came out.

The RSPB in those days was a relatively small society. It had a nominal membership of around 6,000 but as people were kept on the books until they were about two and a half years in arrears with their subscriptions, I daresay that the paid-up membership was not much above three or four thousand compared with the 25,000 plus of today. It was, therefore, less easy to recruit voluntary watchers, but enthusiasm

4

was certainly not lacking and I hope it is not simply my grizzled hairs which cause me to say that most of the watchers had to do a job of work under tiresome conditions and it was never intended that they should necessarily enjoy themselves. I am bound to say that nowadays bird-watching apparently always has to be fun; most people seem to be quite incapable of cooking for themselves and have to be attracted by union hours and the promise of at least one or two days off a week. Things were very different in 1948 when I had to organise a small band of volunteers to safeguard the avocets which it was hoped would breed at both Minsmere and Havergate. In the event, the birds had deserted Minsmere and moved to Havergate and Orfordness. All we had was one tent pitched on uncomfortable shingle. We had inimitable deflatable Lilo mattresses and blankets, a single Primus stove for our cooking and a tea-chest as a larder. Many things, including bread, were still rationed. I think my best companions were my good friends J. K. Stanford and Dick Wolfendale, who subsequently became the warden at Minsmere. There were seldom more than two of us in residence, which was just as well in one small tent. Once it was really dark, we used to turn in and sleep, but one of us was always up at first light, keeping watch on the birds until his companion woke up and made breakfast. Every evening the boatman came down with supplies and a newspaper, but otherwise we were completely cut off. The day was always a long one but when the weather was fine it was comfortable enough. When it rained and the wind blew it could be unpleasant, but it never ceased to be worthwhile.

It is history now that the birds in that particular year were overtaken by a great disaster. Havergate Island was infested with rats. We saw plenty of traces of them but we deliberately kept right away from the shallow salt lagoons amid which the birds had their nests and it never occurred to us that the rats might go out amongst them. True, we occasionally woke up in the dark of the night to hear avocets calling in a state of some agitation, but once we had satisfied ourselves that no intruders were around, we always used to attribute this to an otter or some other creature. But eventually one clutch disappeared, then another and investigation revealed eaten-out egg shells which had been rolled away under cover several feet from the nest. In fact all the first clutches were taken by rats but two or three pairs laid again and in the event three young avocets were successfully reared. I remember it was in the middle of June that we ran out of watchers and I had to take a week on my own. It was a wet summer and I struck atrocious weather, a mixture of heavy rain and wind, sea fog and thunderstorms. I do not think that I was ever completely dry day or night during the whole week that I was in residence and yet I would not hesitate to have it all over again if I could only be given the chance.

From those small beginnings, Havergate Island has developed into one of the most important bird reserves of the RSPB. It is relatively very small and completely surrounded by water, which makes it comparatively easy to keep free from disturbance. At about the same time Minsmere, so close but so very different, was being developed. This was a large area of 1,500 acres, partly woodland and partly heathland, but also with a 300-acre marsh slowly changing from saline to fresh water and with reed-beds growing up apace round numerous shallow lagoons. Nearly 100 species breed on this incredible area and up to 200 are recorded annually by the warden. In the late '40's and early '50's, however, the Society was not wealthy enough to afford even one full-time warden and it was necessary to switch Dick Wolfendale, who normally looked after a small endowed sanctuary in Cheshire, down to Minsmere every summer, where he lived happily in the relatively primitive conditions of a small hut. I have the highest admiration and respect for Dick, who was not a young man at the time but who appeared to me to be as tough as they come and who had two of the great virtues of a warden – patience and tact. It is worth mentioning that on one occasion during my secretaryship of the RSPB I had a letter from a gentleman in Yorkshire enclosing a cheque and stating that he wished to become a member because he had been extremely impressed by the firm but tactful way in which Dick had thrown him out when he had attempted to enter Minsmere bird reserve with his wife without either of them having permits.

My period of sole responsibility for RSPB reserves was comparatively short, since in 1952 I was appointed secretary. But one of the things which I had always found to be essential was the provision of reasonable facilities for visitors. In this idea I came up against the opposition of more than one member of the council, not least the one whom I respected most. I would be the last person to deny the basic principle that reserves must be subject only to the most limited disturbance if they are to succeed; on the other hand, I believe it is quite impossible to expect people to subscribe sums of money unless they are to be allowed some facilities for discovering how and why it is spent. Besides, my own feeling is that the best reason for preserving wild life is so that we can enjoy it. A fairly effective compromise was reached by erecting a number of hides into which visitors could be introduced and, incidentally, get much better views of birds than they would have done if they had wandered about all over the place.

Those post-war years in America as well as in Britain produced a tremendous upsurge of interest in wild life in general and birds in particular. In fact, bird-watching became a vogue; much of it, to tell the truth, was not even distantly related to ornithology and there were inevitably plenty of people to claim that the currency was being debased. There was something in this argument but with the trend so generally beneficial to bird conservation I, for one, have no doubt that it had its merits. It was fostered by radio programmes, not least by a programme which appeared every month under the title of 'Birds in Britain', chaired by James Fisher, than whom birds have never had a more ebullient advocate. A lot of ideas good and bad were cribbed from the USA, especially the competitive notion of tally hunting.

There is something more than a mere undercurrent of dissatisfaction between the ornithologist who is anxious to add, in some way or another, to our knowledge of birds and their habits, and the bird-watcher, who may be largely out for the exercise, the fresh-air and the fun of the thing. But whether we like it or not, most people will always remain in the latter class. It may be partly due to inclination or ability but, more often than not, it may be a matter of time. In any event, there seems to me much to be said for enjoying any innocent recreation in the open-air provided no harm is done to other people or interests.

The famous Boxing Day bird-counts organised by the Audubon

societies in America were amongst the pioneer efforts in the organised 'have fun' hierarchy. Their value may be largely confined to propaganda in favour of birds but, apart from the fact that there is virtue in enabling people to enjoy themselves, they would not appear to hold the potential dangers inherent in relatively scientific efforts like the regular checking up on nests in the breeding season and in ringing and banding. Nobody can say with any certainty that inspecting nests results in any great harm but it cannot be said to do any good either, for in the nesting season birds do best with the minimum of interference: if it were not so, little purpose would be served by limiting access and controlling visitors to bird reserves. And although ringing was persistently 'whitewashed' by its disciples, in Britain, at least, there is now general agreement that it ought to be controlled by law and organised on a permit basis. If it had not been for the rigorous control exercised by the British Trust for Ornithology in recent years the position would have been worse than it is and at the moment there is nothing to prevent a small child from procuring colour-rings and trapping birds, though admittedly the chances of this happening are slight. I am not a ringer: to that extent anything which I say is apt to be biased. Yet some of my own personal experiences have been somewhat disquieting.

Many years ago, after speaking to a well-known bird-society in the Midlands, a film was shown by a member who had recently been to Scotland. His party had discovered a brood of young sandpiper chicks, about a week or ten days old, and a film-record had been made of how one of the brood had been pursued over the stones beside a half-dry river in order that it could be caught and ringed. The chick was filmed scrambling desperately over the rough ground. When it stumbled gusts of laughter swept through the audience. The sequence seemed almost interminable, the tiring but desperate bird summoning up just sufficient energy to evade the capturing hand at the last moment. When it was finally caught the hilarity ceased whilst the attentive audience watched the light metal ring being efficiently put round the leg and then the young creature was put down, oh, so gently, on the stones. How far it was from the rest of the family one could only guess. Whether it survived or not I do not know but it did at least have the honour of serving science and the insatiable desire for public entertainment simultaneously. If it did succumb it did not die wholly in vain, for the idiotic laughter of that gormless bird-loving audience taught me a lesson which I trust I shall never forget.

One other ringing experience is worth mentioning. It occurred many years ago, when I was taking part in mounting a guard over the Scottish ospreys. I had gone on watch late in the evening with a companion. I had left the hide for a few minutes to wander into a shallow copse of young pines nearby. A low sun was still shining and glinted momentarily on an object ahead of me and I was lucky enough to be looking down at the ground just at the right moment. Further investigation revealed a ringed chaffinch, about ten days old, which ought still to have been in a nest. Looking round, I discovered a second fledgling, also newly-ringed, only a few feet away. The birds were still very much alive, so I hunted for and found the nest, which was in a fork of a young fir about eight or nine feet from the ground. I clambered up and found two more ringed chicks in the nest. Carefully putting my two charges on top of them, I held the palm of my hand over the nest for a few minutes until they had settled down, then quietly withdrew.

Full of righteous (or so I hope) wrath, I conducted an inquiry at breakfast next morning and discovered to my dismay that the culprit was a member of my own staff on the RSPB. To give him credit, he was terribly penitent. It had been impossible to tell, looking at the nest from below, how old the young chicks were. Yet when he did discover them he should have refrained from trying to ring them but ringers, like bird-photographers and other friends of birds (and remember that, ninety-nine times out of a hundred, their *goodwill* is unimpeachable), do sometimes lack the will to resist temptation. But this is no proper excuse for such conduct, quite apart from the fact that ringing conducted on such lines is bound to give false results.

Yet incidents of this kind, though disquieting, have little bearing upon conservation as a whole, concerned, as they usually are, with common species. Bird-photographers can cause much more damage. In this field we all too often find the rarity factor almost as great an obsession as it can be with the died-in-the-wool type of egg-collector. If photographers have done great service to wild life in general and to birds in particular, by making the public much more aware of nature through the press and on television, there is equally no question that a good many of them must have uneasy consciences.

There is a story (which I have endeavoured to kill in print before) that two well-known photographers once caused the only pair of goshawks known to be nesting in England to desert. It has been said that the female abandoned the nest because a pylon hide was erected. I knew of that particular nest and, to the best of my knowledge and belief, the bird had either deserted or been shot before any action was taken by the photographers. But it is not irrelevant to point out that these two photographers had every intention of erecting their hide, for no better purpose than to try to obtain pictures of the only known English pair of goshawks. Some risk was obviously entailed in the project. It was perfectly feasible to secure photographs, as many people have done, in countries where the species is (or was) tolerably common. The desire to photograph a really rare species is little more reputable than the itch which drives the kleptomaniac egg-collector.

There is the classic and well-authenticated story of a medical doctor who put up a hide beside a haystack in which a yellow wagtail had its nest. In order to get good shots of the parents feeding the young, some of the hay was pulled aside to expose the nest. On concluding operations for the day the doctor pushed the surroundings of the nest back so effectively that the birds were unable to feed their chicks. One only hopes that this individual displays more intelligence in his treatment of his patients than in the birds which are unlucky enough to be his photographic targets.

Many years ago, when he was a very young man, a well-known ornithologist took up bird photography and began, as is all too-often the case, by tackling rarities. One of his first targets was a bittern on a coastal marsh in East Anglia. Over a weekend he put up his hide close to a nest but also within view of a frequented public-footpath. He left it to return to work, intending to come back on the following Saturday to get his pictures. Perhaps he did: if so, it might be as well to take this opportunity to apologise to him for the absence of his hide. There was a somewhat similar sequel when another individual trespassed on to the Minsmere reserve of the RSPB and put up a hide at a stone curlew's nest on a remote part of the heathland. This hide was subsequently discovered by Major Esmond Lynn-Allen, sportsman and conservationist, who was then living at Scot's Hall, a house which is actually in the reserve. That particular hide was dismantled and buried. Bitterns and stone curlews are rare birds in Britain, protected by special penalties under the Protection of Birds Act. Yet the law does nothing – so far, anyway – to protect them from the selfish whims of bird-photographers: when one does wreck a hide in one's anger I suspect that one may well be breaking the law oneself.

I have on my own conscience (amongst many other things, alas!) the fact that I was once indirectly responsible for the wrecking of a merlin's nest. I was with a film-unit which had better remain nameless. I had no particular interest in the filming at that precise time and was, in point of fact, enjoying a holiday in the Scottish highlands with two or three friends. Knowing that the cameraman was desperately in need of 'personalities' we had found him a ring-ouzel's nest but otherwise we had left him to it, for he was working and we were playing. Then, coming off the hills late one evening of a fine June day, we stumbled across a merlin's nest in the heather. The eyass flew round above us with petulant cries of alarm. We looked for just long enough to notice that at least two of the handsome eggs were well-chipped before we left her to it.

I spent a good deal of that night wondering whether or not to tell the film-maker of my discovery. I did tell him, but subsequent events made me wish that I had kept my great big mouth tightly shut. After breakfast four of us set out, the photographer weighed down with his gear, in spite of the fact that we were all sharing a part of his burden. We reached the foot of the slope on the side of which and perhaps two or three hundred yards away the sitting merlin was concealed. It was a warm morning with a cloudless sky. I had laid down certain stipulations, the most important of which was that the photographer was not to spend more than fifteen minutes near the nest at the most and I expressed the hope that he would get his hide securely erected in ten.

Two of us remained at the foot of the slope, one member of the party helping the cameraman up the slope with his load. There was, of course, no intention of undertaking any photography that day. As the two men approached the spot the bird flew off and I started my timing. Within two or three minutes the friend who had carried some gear up for the photographer had scrambled back downhill to join us and we settled back on a bank.

To cut a long story short, the photographer spent fifty-five minutes close to the nest fiddling with and erecting the hide, moving it to one or two different sites, with two newly-hatched chicks lying, exposed to full sunshine, in the nest only a few yards from him, whilst the female merlin, having cried her heart out for a few minutes, had retreated to perch on a boulder. I know now that, long before the hour had passed, I should have gone up that slope and pulled the photographer out of it, together with his confounded hide. Yet I could not believe he would break our original bargain and I kept on thinking that he must be just on the point of returning.

The photographer, when at last I had the chance to express my views on his behaviour, pleaded that he had had no idea that he had been near the nest for more than about a quarter of an hour, that he had been completely absorbed in his job of erecting the hide and then moving it to various sites near the nest in order to get the best view of it and also to get the light right at the period of the day when he was mostly likely to undertake photography, and so on, adding, apologetically enough, that he had never really had the chance to keep a check on the time: although he had a wrist-watch he had really been so preoccupied and so anxious to get away from the nest at the earliest possible moment. I believe that every word he said was perfectly true. But he never got his film-sequences. The nest and young all came to grief. The worst egg-collector could not have ensured a greater or more complete disaster.

In all fairness I hasten to add that I have had experience of a number of bird photographers and, almost without exception, when rules and regulations have been laid down they have adhered to them with good grace, even granted that they were not in a position to do otherwise. My own considered opinion is that photography of rare birds, unless they are known to be very amenable species, is best undertaken with a neutral person to make the rules and act as referee in seeing that they are obeyed. All too often bird photographers are limited in the amount of time which they have available for the job. Even if an individual knows perfectly well that it is unreasonable to keep a bird off for longer than a very few minutes and that he ought to remove a hide if a bird fails to return to a nest reasonably quickly, there is an understandable if inexcusable temptation to give the thing 'just a few more minutes': it is just those few minutes which so often make all the difference to the success or otherwise of the bird.

It would be unfair to put the irresponsible bird ringer or bird photographer into the pillory without mentioning bird watchers, who certainly contain quite as high an irresponsible element and who are in any event vastly more numerous and growing year by year. Untold harm is undoubtedly done by people who insist on prowling about for no better reason than to find nests, not always only to satisfy an understandable though not always excusable curiosity, but as part of the game of what has come to be known as one-upmanship. In spite of the fact that some of the most rewarding studies of birds have been made on common species, sometimes almost in the back garden, there is a strange snobbery in existence which rests upon the number of species one has seen in one's lifetime. As one's success in this rather puerile competition must depend largely upon the opportunities which one has, any merit it contains must be very dubious, to say the least. I was once in a hide on Havergate Island in Suffolk and had been watching a comparatively rare passage migrant there, a little stint, with the warden, Reg Partridge. On a lovely sun-lit August day the little bird had been walking up and down on the edge of the mud almost immediately in front of us, but then a little pack of dunlin swept past and the stint joined them and flew with them to settle on the far side of the lagoons, and was no longer distinguishable from its companions, not so much because of the distance as for the intense shimmering heat haze. Shortly afterwards three or four visitors entered the hide and the warden pointed out how unfortunate it was that they had not come earlier and got fine views of the little stint. The newcomers were dismayed because none of them had ever seen one before. When the warden pointed out the little group of dunlin far off in the haze and said that among them there was almost certainly a little stint, at least two of the visitors, without being in any way able to distinguish it, got out their little note-books and added it to their growing list of 'lifers'. Of course it can be argued that all this is very harmless but it is stupid, too, and singularly futile when it comes to the problems of conservation. How much better if those Havergate visitors had been doing a worthwhile job of work acting as voluntary wardens on some reserve, or guarding some species like the osprey. Or would it be a drawback today in that 100,000 British people have got the osprey on their life tally, even though some of them would be incapable of recognising a chaffinch or a wood pigeon.

Having enjoyed almost every minute of my own life I am reluctant to criticise any form of fun. I have already indicated that the tally hunters do not do very much harm any way; at least their sympathies are on the right side. The more scientific bird-watcher can often be a much greater menace. Since the black-tailed godwit started to breed in East Anglia in 1952, it has been impossible to disclose the site simply because the rubber-necking bird-watchers are regarded as too great a menace to be worth the risk. In a recent issue of *British Birds* there was a record of a pair of black-tailed godwits which had apparently attempted to nest on a west-country marsh in 1963. The ornithologists who reported this record had behaved in a manner which seems to me still to be almost incredible. Having located the birds in June, they discovered that the adults were behaving in a way which made them believe that they had young. They then went on to say that in spite of intensive searches, the chicks were never found. I find it difficult to believe that it was not realised that to conduct any sort of a search, intensive or otherwise, might well lead to tragedy. It is this kind of example that makes one despair for the cause of the rare bird. Yet, oddly enough, even the best of us is apt at times to make our own rules.

When I was with the RSPB there was at one time a member of the council (and one for whom, incidentally, I had a high regard) who, if he had had his way, would scarcely have allowed any visitors on any bird reserve under any circumstances whatsoever. Yet when, soon after the godwits had returned to East Anglia and there were only three or four pairs present, I took him down to see them with two colleagues, he did not hesitate to insist upon doing something which we had never done, which was to go out in an attempt to find a nest. Circumstances alter cases. Perhaps it was ever thus.

I intend to discuss recent developments in legislation for the protection of birds in the next chapter, but this may be as good a place as any to mention the fact that proposals are now afoot to endeavour to prohibit the wilful disturbance of rare nesting species. At the present moment, whilst one cannot legally destroy a rare bird like the golden eagle, or take its eggs, no offence would be committed if by some means or another one deliberately prevented the bird from brooding her eggs.

It seems doubtful, however, if such a cause is worthy of a virtually unenforceable piece of legislation, but it would also perhaps thwart the over enthusiastic bird-photographer or even the over curious bird-watcher. It is difficult to see, however, at what point one could say that interference has been deliberate. Few bird-photographers ever expect any bird to desert; in fact if it does so they have successfully cut off their noses to spite their faces. It is the sort of thing which is likely to be of greater benefit to lawyers than to breeding birds. What of course is really required is much more education for those who in theory at least are supposed to be educated and a much greater sense of discipline in the bird-watching and protection societies, whether at national or local level. The Wildfowlers Association of Great Britain and Ireland does not hesitate not only to expel a member who has broken the law or through bad sportsmanship may have brought the Association into disrepute, but they also publish his name and address. Education without discipline is not education at all.

Education is obviously essential before anybody can hope to understand any subject. It has become a parrot cry in conservation to say that education is the most rewarding long-term policy. Few people ever define the term and it is always important to consider who precisely is going to do the teaching. It is a fact, not necessarily a healthy one, but unavoidable under all the circumstances, that in the modern world more and more young people are growing up in urban areas. Inevitably they tend to be introduced to rural topics and wild life by people who are not countrymen, who, understandably enough, regard the countryside as a sort of recreational playground, and who, with the best intentions in the world, are ill-qualified for the task. A town child interested in birds may well, for instance, feel that shooting cannot possibly be related to conservation – quite the contrary in fact. Who is going to explain to a youngster the part which sport has played both in the conservation and the destruction of wild life? Probably some good-natured man or woman who has not only never done any shooting but knows absolutely nothing at first hand of the part which this sport has played in the whole development of the rural scene. This problem I believe to be a very real one, and it applies just as much in the United States or the Netherlands or any other country as it does in Britain. All too often, when conservationists begin to think of educating the young, they think in terms of propaganda which is often especially suspect because it is subject to the limited experience of the individual. Nature should always be respected, but never worshipped.

When it comes to young people we should perhaps try to clarify our minds as to what precisely we are trying to do. Obviously it will be impossible to interest them in the problems of wild life conservation unless one can not only give them some interest in the flora and fauna, and at least for a limited period, and perhaps also in a limited way, encourage them to take some active part.

In 1943 the RSPB launched its Junior Bird Recorders' Club. This was not only a bold thing to do in the middle of a war, but it attracted a very considerable membership amongst young people between the ages of 11 and 18 years. No doubt the majority of these were fairly inactive participants (which is true of almost any organisation), but it published an informative magazine, encouraged its members to keep records and it ran a long series of extremely successful annual conferences which were quite as much of an education to the organisers as to the students. This club has now been renamed the Young Ornithologists Club and there is no lower age limit, though too much should not be read into this rather high-flown title. Ornithologists grow from perambulators no doubt, yet relatively few conduct scientific observations from them.

But good as these sort of organisations may be in fostering some kind of an interest in birds and their welfare, I believe they have two basic failings. The first and perhaps the least important is that they tend to make young people almost too intense. Childhood and youth are a time when there is so much to see and to learn and so much to enjoy that I doubt the value, even perhaps the morality, of trying to mould a young mind to think along the lines along which you want it to think. At least it ought to be given every opportunity of thinking differently. I can perhaps make my point a little clearer by going back forty years or more to the days when nature study figured in the curriculum of many schools. Many of my generation, even though they are now keen naturalists, shudder at the memory, and perhaps the astonishing thing is that one's interest survived this ordeal. It is true that today the same sort of thing is taught in a more lively way – at least we like to think so. But this brings me to the second point which I wanted to make, which is that I think our approach to the whole subject is almost always too narrow. Leaving aside the fact that birds are a relatively small and not especially important aspect of nature, it seems vital that natural history should not be hived off as if it existed in some completely watertight compartment with no particular value to man, unless he chooses to poke his nose into it. Many youngsters still grow up with the idea that a piece of woodland is just a pleasant piece of scenery perhaps full of birds and beasties, but without the slightest idea that it is a crop which, like a corn field, must be harvested at the right time unless it is to be wasted. Few of them, I think, would be likely to learn that the woodland was the home for pheasants which the landowner and his friends would enjoy shooting in the winter. They might not be told that without this sporting interest, not only would the wood perhaps not be there at all, but the pheasants might not be there either.

The extreme protectionist may well shudder at the whole idea but it is impossible to deny that sport and conservation have gone together for generations, even if until fairly recently they have been unwilling to acknowledge one another. Certainly it is no job of the conservationist to start moralising upon the ethics of field sports when educating young people. Given the facts and the opportunities, they can in due course make up their own minds. Let them have the facts and let them, if possible, enjoy the experience of trying things for themselves.

Birds do exist, though usually in limited numbers and variety, in large conurbations, but it would be fair to say that they belong to the country and are a part of it. To concentrate one's entire interest upon a small and limited aspect of that countryside does not seem to me to be very intelligent. What I believe is required above all else is to foster a genuine interest in the countryside as a whole because, unless that countryside is preserved to the best of our ability and every allowance made for all its various interests, economic, recreational, aesthetic and so forth, conservation will ultimately fail.

We talk glibly about our responsibility to pass on to our children and grandchildren our national heritage and yet there are plenty of people who spend a considerable part of their time fostering arguments between the very people who for one reason or another are desperately anxious to try to do precisely that. Opponents of field sports, for instance (whatever other merits they may have), are no friends of conservation. You may or may not approve of stag hunting on Exmoor, and you equally well may be quite prepared to express a very forcible opinion even if you have never seen a staghound or Exmoor. What is a fact is that if it were not for stag hunting on Exmoor, the red deer would have been exterminated – and not by humane methods either. If we really want to preserve the countryside and wild life, certainly in highly civilised countries, it is surely common prudence that all those who are genuinely interested in doing this, from any angle, should pool their resources and their strength. Bearing in mind that at least eighty per cent of the population probably doesn't care a brass farthing one way or the other, unity seems a first essential and it is one which should never be lost sight of for a moment when it comes to interesting (which is a much better word than teaching) the younger generation. What about the vast masses who go into the countryside and despoil it with beer bottles, cigarette cartons and other litter? It is all very well to be horrified but if one goes to some of the industrial slums of Yorkshire or Lancashire or the Midlands and sees for oneself the sort of horizon which is the daily accompaniment of the lives of many of these people, one really ought to think again. Even when most of these people do get into the country they probably sit in a box on wheels seeing little and hearing less, their eyes fixed on the vehicle ahead. Granted that it would be fatal if all these people started to take to their legs and walked all over the countryside, the basic problem remains that we cannot begin to get people to appreciate the value of natural scenery and wild life unless it can somehow be made real to them.

Whether television is the answer is at least open to doubt. A noble lord in Parliament recently suggested that there was no need for little boys to go birds-nesting or even to observe wild life at all; all they had to do was to watch natural history programmes on their 19-inch screen, introduced by Peter Scott. It all sounds to me very unconvincing, rather like suggesting that I can live on bread and milk and potatoes and get my pleasure from watching somebody on television eating oysters and roast partridge. Seriously, however, this is the sort of level at which a great many people are thinking today, and, so far as wild life is concerned, it is very, very sad.

5 Legislation – Safeguard or Shibboleth?

One way in which protection can be given to birds is through legislation. In Britain at least some sort of limited local protection of this kind has in fact been in existence in some form or another for centuries, but all the earliest legislation sprang from attempts to assist sporting interests. Those people who have little interest in or who may even actively object to field sports should realise that some of this legislation, limited as it was, benefited some birds which either through lack of interest or lack of local protection or perhaps a combination of the two, have since suffered badly. As long ago as the reign of Henry VIII and probably earlier, many of the birds of prey, especially the falcons, were accorded strong protection by the law in the interests of the sport of falconry. This, one of the most ancient and certainly one of the most natural and skilful of all field sports, has long been in decline, partly because it is a great art and the training of falcons requires endless patience and partly because in recent years agricultural developments and enclosures have made it extraordinarily difficult for the falconer to fly his birds, save in a few favoured areas. In the old days falconry was very much a sport practised by royalty and the aristocracy. It is therefore not surprising that such laws as existed to protect and preserve falcons had really stiff penalties attached to them. It seems impossible really to tell now how effective their enforcement was, but certainly if there was any real risk of being caught out, there can be no doubt that the penalties should have acted as a very considerable deterrent to the would-be offender. Thus in the middle ages, and for two or three hundred years thereafter, it seems likely that most birds of prey flourished in Britain to a degree which has never since been paralleled. It should be added, however, that it would be a mistake to attribute the abundance of a bird like the red kite during that period either to the interest in falconry or to the laws which supported it, though the kite, which was regarded as a useful scavenger in the days before dustmen (refuse disposal operatives), was given some legal status.

The arrival of the muzzle-loading shotgun marked the beginning of an age when birds like pheasants and partridges and wildfowl took on a new value for sportsmen. In Britain the Game Act of 1831, for instance, gave strong legal protection to birds like grouse, black game, pheasants and partridges as well as to snipe and woodcock. Although there have been one or two amending or supporting acts directly related to the Game Act of 1831, the original act still remains the cornerstone of legal protection for what may loosely be described as game birds as distinct from wildfowl. It is not difficult to see why, generally speaking, legislation for the protection of game birds was pretty effective. Although in recent years they may have been thinner on the ground than they once were, gamekeepers have always been available to look after their charges, and, since trespassing in pursuit of game is an offence, keepers have been in a much stronger position to enforce the law than have the wardens of bird reserves. Public sympathy, too, has been pretty solidly behind legislation designed to protect game – or at least that small proportion of the public who displayed any interest in the matter one way or the other.

Many people will be puzzled at the slow and generally ineffective way in which legislation for the protection of birds, other than sporting birds, has developed. This is attributable to a number of reasons. The current interest in wild life and in the preservation of natural scenery has no parallel in any previous century. If the threats to scenery were nothing like as great as they are today, the pressures on wild life were developing rapidly even as early as the end of the eighteenth century.

Yet it is only necessary to read the letters of Gilbert White to realise that in those days when any curious bird was destroyed on sight, the supply of most animals was regarded as inexhaustible.

Another cause of the slow development of legislation for the protection of wild birds has, I think, been largely due to the fact that public opinion has for so long either been largely misinformed or not informed at all. Despite their many virtues, democratic governments only get into power by courtesy of the majority of the electorate and, for good or ill, the general principle is one man one vote, lunatics and peers of the realm excepted. However undesirable it may be, it would seem that few political parties can indulge themselves very far in considering the wishes of minorities and even today in Britain the people with any real interest in the preservation of wild life are still only a very small minority. This is in itself an important reason why there should be goodwill and understanding between such people, whether their interest springs from an interest in sport or natural history, or, as is more generally the case, a combination of the two.

Before we examine the pattern of legislation in more detail, it should also be remarked that in Britain at least (and America amongst other countries has been more fortunate in this respect) successive governments of all political shades have shown little or no interest in promoting laws directed solely towards the preservation of the countryside and its wild life. The excuse usually advanced is that parliamentary time is too fully occupied with more important matters. Going round Britain in the 1960's and seeing what has happened to much of the coastline, one is entitled to wonder whether this excuse is in any way reasonable. Most of the legislation for the protection of birds has been introduced by way of private Members' bills, either in the House of Commons or the House of Lords. Almost the maximum that any government has ever been able to do, at any rate in recent years, has been to regard such bills with benevolence. It is important to realise just what this means in terms of actually doing something.

In 1947 I was one of a number of people appointed by the Home Secretary to a committee whose task was to review existing legislation for the protection of birds and to draft the basis of a new Act. In fact many years earlier a similar committee had been working on this very problem, since it had become very evident that the original Act of 1880 with its many amending or subsidiary acts had become so involved and archaic that it was purely decorative. The outbreak of the Second World War had inevitably interrupted the whole process so that in 1947 the new committee started off from scratch. This committee was a highly representative one, including sportsmen as well as protectionists and, quite apart from its main work, I believe it did a great deal to start the movement which has resulted in the healing of a very serious breach which had previously developed between them. If, being now as grey as a badger, I may pontificate for a moment, I would say that in my experience a great number of the differences which develop between people, whether individually or through organised groups, are often largely due to misunderstanding.

I cannot now remember how many sittings of that post-war committee were held, but I think that we met at least two or three times a year and it was four or five years before our deliberations ended and we were able to submit our proposals to the Secretary of State. That there were some minor disagreements must be evident from the later debates in Parliament, but so far as I was concerned I was most agreeably surprised, not only at the friendly relations which developed between all of us, but by the universal agreement which was reached in the solution of the great majority of the many problems which beset us. I must confess to two characteristics which are not, I hope, vices, but which are not necessarily always virtues either. I am impatient and I am an optimist. I believe my impatience arises from the fact that I think that time is very seldom on anybody's side, either on the wider historical scale or even in the lifetime of an individual. If we have an average span of seventy years, it seems to me it is little enough and of those twenty years are spent in growing up; that leaves us fifty in which only a little more than half give most of us the inestimable advantage of some experience to supply us with prudent common sense and the physical powers which may be necessary to push ourselves along at full strength. As to being an optimist I suppose my feelings here spring from a marriage of genuine enjoyment of life and a suspicion that on any other basis our complicated existence might be scarcely bearable.

My mention of these personal matters is necessary in order to understand my intense personal disappointment when having given my services (for what they were worth) on a committee of the Home Office for several years, it became apparent that the government of the day were not particularly interested in the results nor had they any intention of giving up any parliamentary time to implement our proposals. If our labours were to be productive of anything at all, it would once again have to be through a private Members' bill, though, with certain reservations, it appeared that our recommendations would have the government's blessing. For those who may not know what the procedure in connection with private Members' bills is, it had better be explained that at the beginning of each parliamentary session in November, bills which M.P.s may wish to promote are taken on the basis of a lottery. As only one day a fortnight is devoted to these measures, only those which come first out of the hat can have any real chance of reaching the statute book, because any bills which are still in the pipeline or which have not been started upon when the session concludes at the end of the following summer are technically killed and, if they are not forgotten altogether, must take their place in the next State sweepstake.

It fell to Lady Tweedsmuir to introduce into Parliament what was to become the Protection of Birds Act 1954. She won an excellent position in the 1953–54 session and piloted the bill into port with skill and graciousness that placed all bird protectionists eternally in her debt. Yet there were a number of snags and difficulties. The committee to which I have already referred was in no two minds about the necessity to make any new legislation as simple as possible if it were to have any reasonable hope of being understood and enforced. It is not only a question of the public themselves being able to understand legislation, but it is equally, if not more important, that those who must undertake the responsibility of enforcing it, e.g. the police force and magistrates, should be able to do so too.

Trouble arose almost at the outset over a point which may seem trivial enough in itself but which was really of the utmost importance.

The basic idea behind the new Act was very sound in that all birds and their eggs would be protected unless the Act subsequently stated otherwise. This was a complete reversal of the previous legislation, where all birds which were protected had to be specifically named. Worse still, under the old legislation individual counties had been able to make their own Orders, subject to the ultimate approval of the Home Secretary or the Secretary of State for Scotland. This led to absurd anomalies such as a rare bird like the hobby being protected in one county but not in an adjacent one, so that if it had a nest near the border between the two, it went in and out of legal protection umpteen times a day. Endless lists of birds were named on official notices which were displayed on police notice boards throughout the country and which must have been utterly meaningless to most people who even bothered to look at them. The fact that a county borough in the south of England listed the red-necked phalarope as one of the species whose eggs could not be taken when there was not in fact such a nest within 500 miles was only one of the many absurdities. The principle behind the new Act abolished all this. The majority of birds are not mentioned at all which means that, with their nests and eggs, they enjoy all the year round protection.

There are four schedules to the Act in which species are named. The first concerns rare or very rare species for which heavier penalties are specifically prescribed in the Act. A very few species are put in a second part to this First Schedule and are not protected outside the close season, either because they are sporting birds but are rare as breeding species in Britain, or because, as in the case of the whimbrel, it might be extremely difficult for a shooter to separate them from a very similar species which may be shot. The Second Schedule includes a short list of birds such as the crow and the wood pigeon which are regarded as pests and which can be destroyed by an owner or occupier or any person authorised by him. Anybody, however, can take the eggs of these species. I mention this because it is an important point that I want to refer to later. The Third Schedule covers a number of sporting birds, mainly duck and geese, but including a few waders such as redshank and curlew, which may be shot between September 1st and January 31st both dates inclusive, with an extension, in the case of duck and geese only, until February 20th below high water mark of ordinary mean tides. (Almost all saltings and green marsh are, incidentally, above this limit and are therefore excepted from this extension.) The Fourth Schedule is a rather specialised one listing birds which may not be sold in captivity and which need not concern us at the moment.

Perhaps no legislation can avoid all anomalies. For instance, whilst it became an offence under Schedule Two for an unauthorised person to trespass upon private land and shoot a magpie, it was not only not an offence under the Act if he came on to that land in May and took a clutch of magpies' eggs, but he was equally at liberty to shoot a wild duck in season and even to walk off with his booty, in spite of any protests the aggrieved landowner might reasonably be expected to make. I doubt if anybody can put up any good reason whatsoever why, if only owners or occupiers or persons authorised by them can destroy pest birds listed in the Second Schedule, all and sundry may take their eggs. This was a singularly stupid and totally unnecessary provision, but far worse was to follow, when the bill came before the House of Commons. There was an immediate and almost hysterical outcry to the effect that if the eggs of almost all birds were protected, egg-collecting boys would become criminals. The Secretary of State, at the time Sir David Maxwell-Fyfe (now Lord Kilmuir) was one of the first to support this view, not only in the face of the most persistent warnings by his Advisory Committee, but also in spite of the fact that for years successive Home Secretaries had been putting their signatures to County Council Orders which did precisely the same thing. Objectors claimed that, if the eggs of many relatively common birds were protected, innocent children would lose their legal innocence. This was a technical objection that, quite frankly, would have been better left to the discretion of the courts. There is nothing at all in the Litter Act which absolves a baby in a perambulator from offending against its provisions and not becoming at least a technical criminal if it throws a bit of paper on to the pavement, and I should be delighted if any Member of Parliament can tell me what legal right a small child has to ride a tricycle on the sidewalk. Surely any responsible society and those responsible for administering its laws must always retain some sense of proportion. However, in case everybody is not in agreement with me on this point, let us see just how this piece of farcicality actually ended up.

In order not to delay the passage of the bill through Parliament, the Secretary of State gave an assurance that he would seek advice and make an Order, one applicable to England and Wales and one applicable to Scotland, which would list a number of birds from whose eggs the protection otherwise afforded to them would be withdrawn. A list of thirteen species was eventually drawn up for England and Wales and a few more in Scotland. So it became legal for little boys (and anybody else of any age) to take and smash or blow and keep eggs of birds like the robin, song thrush, blackbird, chaffinch, wren and skylark; yet there were many common birds whose eggs remained protected, such as those of the yellowhammer. I have no idea whether Lord Kilmuir and many other people who insisted upon this action had ever collected eggs in their boyhood or whether or not they knew anything about the healthy activities of country boys. But the fact is that birds-nesting boys often have very little idea of the identity of many of the eggs which they take. I suppose that Parliament in its wisdom or otherwise considered all this to be very reasonable but it carried with it a corollary which it is perhaps fortunate that the ordinary citizen was not unreasonable enough to try to enforce. This was that having given specific exemption for small boys in relation to a very limited number of species, Parliament must surely have intended that if any boy took an egg outside that list, he was in fact one of the nebulous 'criminals'. I do not propose to say here what I would think of any politician who would seriously consider that a child of ten who took the eggs of a yellowhammer, probably in all innocence, was a criminal, but whatever his party, I would never vote ever again for such a nincompoop.

The real disaster arising from this exemption from protection of certain common birds' eggs lay, however, in the fact that it made it infinitely more difficult to enforce the Act. True, that there were already a number of birds in the Second Schedule whose eggs could be taken by all and sundry (though a little forethought could have avoided this, without in any way helping pest birds, by limiting action to owners, occupiers and authorised persons). However, most of the small number of species included in this schedule of 'outlaws' were generally ones which were fairly easy to distinguish. Those included in the new list – the so-called schoolboys' charter – were in a quite different category and succeeded in confusing the issue so effectively that there was not the slightest hope of the police ever being able to do very much by way of enforcement.

But the play was to be a genuine three-acter, funny from first to last. Every organisation with any interest in this matter had made their opposition clear, but politicians when they are riding high horses take a lot of knocking down. It was not until the very severe winter of 1962–63 decimated a great number of birds, including most of those included in the schoolboys' charter, that an opportunity occurred to attack Parliament by the back door. A hullabaloo was kicked up, pointing out that now that these so-called common birds were at least relatively uncommon, they ought to be put on the protected list forthwith and that even schoolboy collecting might tip the scales against them. Of course this was nonsense except possibly in areas in the immediate vicinity of cities and towns (although even there cats are probably much more effective in controlling the numbers of small birds than any child collectors would ever be). There was not a shred of evidence to suggest that the scale of collecting by boys would in itself have any adverse effect on the recovery of the numbers of the birds. However, some good speeches were made and, for what reason I do not know, Parliament took the bait. True, the general idea was that the Orders would only be rescinded and schoolboys made into criminals for a period of two or three years, but the Secretaries of State, if not the government as a whole, had at last succeeded in putting themselves in an untenable position. Nobody can go on playing the fool for ever and the conservation organisations did not fail to press home their attacks. It is true that at the moment of writing the original Act has not been amended and there is technically nothing to prevent the Secretaries of State from making another Order tomorrow, but the British Government have virtually conceded defeat. When Lord Hurcomb recently introduced a private bill amending the Act in the House of Lords, a provision which would deprive the Home Secretaries of any powers to proscribe the eggs of common birds from protection was agreed virtually without opposition. As all this was no doubt inspired by the Home Office, the wheel has come full circle and Parliament has, so to speak, given itself the kick in the pants that any intelligent conservationist has been trying so hard to administer for the last ten years. So time passes and opportunities are lost; when modern politicians like to fiddle I fancy that poor old Nero had nothing on them.

I have discussed in some detail what many may regard as a comparatively small matter in connection with the British Protection of Birds Act 1954 because I believe that it will serve to show to what lengths apathy and muddle and sometimes – let's face it – plain downright wrong thinking can go. I doubt the virtue of a form of progress which enables one to put people into space and whirl them round the earth at 17,000 miles an hour when in so many other and often vital ways we are as slow as cart-horses. One thing which it was believed would be stopped by the Act which became law in 1954, was the collecting of eggs of birds at an adult level which, more often than not, involved rare species. So far as dealers were concerned – and several were in practice in Britain at that time – the 1954 Act not only made it illegal to sell the eggs of any protected bird but also to offer or even have the eggs in one's possession for sale. A possible loophole was closed by making barter and exchange the equivalent of sale. There was, of course, nothing to prevent people possessing collections of eggs, many of which were in existence and many of which, strangely enough, had undoubtedly been taken illegally. It is no good, however, worrying about the past. I was at that time Secretary of the RSPB and the Council of the Society were, not unnaturally, impatient for action to be taken. It is, however, one thing to know of an illegal dealer and another thing to catch him out. In the end it became evident that the only thing to do was to negotiate a sale. The first man to be prosecuted in this way was a very well-known dealer in Cheshire who has since died and I do not therefore propose to name him. He was a charming personality and it is perhaps just as well to realise that many of the worst egg-collectors are, generally speaking, otherwise very reasonable and likeable people indeed, whilst conversely one or two of the best conservationists are among the last people whom I personally would wish to entertain in my house for a weekend. Just as there are very likeable gentlemen under cloth caps, so many a disreputable character masquerades under a bowler hat. The Cheshire dealer was caught hook, line and sinker and when the case came to court it was very obvious that he had not got a leg to stand on. But the dealer who may have been very naughty but was a man of some character, carried on unabashed and a few months later he was again caught and convicted. There was a bit of fun in this case because I got a tip off at the RSPB that a couple of German collectors who had been in Scotland (not, I guessed, just looking at the scenery) were travelling south on their return journey and were calling on the dealer with the intention of purchasing a number of eggs, including those of the greenshank, protected under special penalties by the Act.

The problem was to know how one was going to prevent them from doing this, or to intercept them if they did. Fortunately I knew the time and date of the boat by which they were crossing back to the continent from Dover and their names and the number of their car. With a colleague I therefore went down to Dover and tackled the police the evening before the day on which they were due to sail at about 1 p.m. There was, however, no provision in the Act which would enable the police to search their car or to question the men in any way. The only suggestion that they could make was that I should go and talk to H.M. Customs. The police, of course, were absolutely right, though I had argued with them far into the evening that this might be a case where perhaps they could chance their arm, not that I thought it in any way unreasonable that they would not do so. The following morning, however, I found that a customs officer was amenable to a suggestion that he should search their baggage, as in fact he had every right to do. The Germans duly arrived in their car and when they got very angry I realised that we had struck oil. The eggs of the greenshank were located and identified and they were then held by customs on the grounds that they might be vital evidence in a case against the man who had sold them. We even managed to persuade the Germans to sign a voluntary statement that they had purchased the eggs from the dealer. Looking back I doubt the morality of all this but I still do not know what else one could do, though the invidious position in which both the customs officer and the writer put themselves could have been avoided, as I hope to make clear later, if the Act contained adequate provision to secure enforcement. Anyway the RSPB got the dealer into court again and he was duly prosecuted, but as the eggs had been sold they were considered legally to belong to the Germans and so they were returned to them, not that that mattered very much. The offender in these two cases got moderate fines (but nothing like as severe as provided for by the Act), and I have no doubt that he went 'underground' and any further dealing which he did with recognised collectors would have become known only by some absolute fluke.

A second dealer was knocked out of business very promptly as the result of an advertisement offering unspecified eggs for sale. A deal was made which involved a number of eggs. One of the few really strong provisions in the Act is that where a Justice of the Peace is satisfied that there is evidence to show that a person is selling or offering eggs for sale, etc., he may grant a search warrant which can be executed by the police. We were inside that dealer's house in no time. He was actually an old man over seventy and it was anything but fun, though the evidence which we were able to unearth, not only by the discovery of thousands of eggs which he intended to sell but from letters to people with whom he was trading, was certainly a revelation. He had hundreds upon hundreds of terns' eggs which were collected for him by light-house keepers on the east coast of Scotland. He paid them one penny per egg, ready blown and carriage paid by the senders. We found an account sent by the lighthouse keepers for one of the several consignments sent in a single summer, 216 eggs at one penny each – 18s. My sympathy for the age of the dealer was slightly modified when I found that he had marked this account '4 broken eggs, one penny each – 4d' and had clearly subtracted the coppers and sent the keepers 17s. 8d. I might add that he listed these terns' eggs for sale at 8d. each, with a very slight reduction for a whole clutch of either two or three eggs. I asked him what he did when anybody wanted a clutch of two or three eggs (which would imply that they came from the same nest) and he told me without batting an eyelid that he did his best to match the eggs up so that his clients could feel satisfied that they really had been laid by one particular bird.

The police took away over 5,000 eggs, most of which needed identification, but there was also a vast amount of correspondence and it was essential to follow this up without delay. We went nearly half-way across England for the most promising suspect and after obtaining a search warrant were a little disconcerted to find that we had discovered another group of people who were all involved. To cut a long story short, apart from the dealer himself it was finally possible to prosecute about six other persons, five of whom were private collectors. It was this adventure which convinced me beyond all doubt that most egg-collecting which has gone on in Britain for a good many years past has been not only scientifically futile but that some of it has been downright silly. I can certainly say with authority that some of the unusual clutches containing a cuckoo's egg with a very unusual foster-parent are completely bogus, rather like the clutches of terns' eggs already mentioned. In the case of many of the clutches of rare birds' eggs, particularly birds of prey, a lot of it was downright wicked and many of the people responsible most certainly ought to have known better. On the other hand a good deal of it concerned the eggs of common birds and it would be a bold man who could assert that it had done any real harm from the conservation angle. Yet much of it was pretty bogus and sordid. The boy who finds a nest himself must learn something about natural history, but buying eggs through the post carries with it no such advantage.

Most of the people who were prosecuted by the RSPB following these investigations were convicted – in fact I can only remember one case when the prosecution failed and in some ways this was one of the most interesting of the lot. As already mentioned barter and exchange of eggs was ranked with selling or offering for sale, or even having in possession for sale. We discovered correspondence from one individual to another in which it appeared that A was very anxious to acquire one of B's peregrine clutches with which B was reluctant to part. However,

B said that if he would give him a particular clutch of blue raven's eggs he would part with the peregrine's. B then wrote to A and said that he was not going to exchange a pig in a poke and that he would need to see the raven's eggs before he could consider the matter further. A then sent B the raven's eggs and said that he would like to see the peregrine clutch before finally making his decision. B acceded to this request and at the time when this correspondence was discovered, indirectly as a result of the search warrant, each party was in possession of the other's clutch on appro. so to speak. A had certainly made it clear in writing that he was prepared to let B have the raven's clutch in exchange for the peregrine's and B had at least gone as far as to suggest that he was willing to barter if the raven's eggs matched up to certain expectations. The issue at stake was therefore whether this constituted an offer to barter or exchange. The facts were never in dispute but the Bench ruled that there was no evidence to support the contention of the prosecution. The chap who said that life was something of a lottery knew a thing or two!

Some of the defences which were put forward were ingeniously magnificent. In one case where evidence was produced in writing that a man had offered a considerable number of clutches for sale and where the defendant rather sensibly pleaded guilty, he informed the Bench that these were the only eggs he ever intended to sell, that the remainder of those in his possession, by far the majority, were never going to be sold at all. He was keeping them so that they could illustrate a book which he was engaged in writing about birds' eggs. This defence was accepted, but needless to say the book has never appeared, nor did the magistrates even inquire for any evidence from the defendant which might show that he had even started to write it.

Oddly enough, one of the highest penalties ever imposed by a Bench in all these cases was on a man who, to the best of my knowledge and belief, never wavered from the truth when giving evidence on oath. I think he had one or two very good opportunities for lying had he wished to do so and I had the deepest admiration for his dignity and courage in giving straightforward answers and it still grieves me, especially when I recall some of the other cases, that telling the truth did not appear to do him very much good. It is perhaps all too often so, not that this chap did not deserve to be punished. Apart from taking many eggs himself, some of which were of rare species, he also purchased a fair number. Some of his 'buys' were made from a notorious university professor who had plundered rare birds' eggs at home and abroad without ever being caught. Among these were two clutches of dotterel eggs, both taken by the professor in Scotland after the Second World War. But not content with these two clutches this man had taken the first opportunity when he was in Scotland, to gratify what surely is a pretty puerile desire, to have a self-taken clutch. There are probably somewhere between fifty and 100 pairs of dotterel nesting each year in Britain. It is a rare and possibly declining species. The way in which it has been harassed and pillaged by a mere handful of people is a disgrace in a civilised community apart from being a complete antithesis of basic conservation. Oddly enough, quite apart from the fact that the eggs taken by the professor had been taken contrary to the law at that time, there was nothing that could be done to bring this rogue to book. It is a most serious weakness in the Protection of Birds Act that, as with most other legislation dealing with civil offences, a summons must be served on the offender within six months of the commission of the offence. Strenuous efforts have in fact been made to try to get this provision altered, but it is very unlikely that they will succeed. The basic objection, which is a valid one, is that where witnesses are required memories fade as time passes.

All these prosecutions took up a great deal of time and money. In the majority of cases the costs of the prosecution at least equalled, if they did not exceed, the fines which were imposed upon the guilty. I once occupied a cell in a police station in the west country from 10 o'clock in the morning until 2 o'clock the next morning, engaged in the dreary and difficult task of indentifying over 5,000 eggs. There were no data cards but I suppose a good oologist would have identified the lot. I was well satisfied when I had catalogued just about 4,000. I suspect that these prosecutions frightened a lot of the collectors not least because, apart from other things, they really do love to protest their innocence. At any rate there have been no comparable prosecutions of recent years, though there is ample evidence to show that their activities continue almost unabated. I have no doubt that some of them could be caught and brought to book provided a real effort was made to do so. That there are difficulties in the way, however, is beyond dispute, and I suppose some people might object to the methods which I think would have to be employed, for they may savour a little of sharp practice. However, one must bear in mind that worse things are done by the police in bringing evidence against notorious criminals and we all know that during the War, when clothing was rationed, petty servants of the government would go round incognito to see if they could persuade some wicked person to part with a pair of stockings without the necessary coupons. I would not suggest that any ordinary citizen should be encouraged to behave in a way quite so sordid and unpleasant, involving as it apparently often did a deceitful attempt to play upon the sympathetic and better side of the human character.

Some ten years ago I got information on the grape-vine that a notorious collector who lived in the south of England, was going up to Scotland on an egg-collecting expedition at the end of May. As I came by this knowledge in February, I had a bit of elbow room in which to work. I asked a friend of mine to see if he could find out more exactly where this chap was intending to go. It would not be politic to say precisely how we discovered the exact hotel in which he intended to stay and his probable dates of arrival and departure. I then joined forces with Mr George Waterston, the Scottish representative of the RSPB, and we went to see a friendly gamekeeper in the vicinity. We offered him a very reasonable bonus if he could assist us in getting a successful prosecution against the collector and he agreed to this. Later on we approached a detective-sergeant who worked in the county in question and who was interested in birds and after a long parley it was agreed that he should approach his chief to see whether he could be seconded for two or three days, booking in at the same hotel as our egg-collector and behaving as if he were a botanist.

This permission was granted on two very odd conditions. The first one was that the detective-sergeant should be prepared to take these days as part of his leave; the second one was that the RSPB would

A long-eared owl caught in a gin-trap. The bird is legally protected: to set the trap is forbidden. The owl dies, all the same.

Eight buzzards and a merlin decorating a keeper's shed in the West of England pay silent tribute to the impotence of the British Protection of Birds Act 1954 under which they enjoyed complete security.

Two sparrowhawks among the vermin on a keeper's gibbet in East Anglia. The sparrowhawk has now almost vanished from this and other areas. But the use of toxic chemicals, not gamekeepers, is the prime cause.

pay all the costs, including the hotel bill which would be incurred by the police officer – all this in aid of the enforcement of the Protection of Birds Act which Parliament had passed two years earlier and which this innocent citizen thought that it was the duty of the police to enforce. How stupid can one be? Any way the important thing was to catch the collector. A few pounds one way or the other would not make much difference if success were achieved and the sergeant was sporting enough to agree to sacrifice what was a considerable portion of his leave to help us. Plenty of self-styled protectionists have done much less. The whole thing went off rather better than we expected. The English collector went first of all to the north of Scotland and then came south to the hotel almost exactly on time. The keeper was able to inform George Waterston at once of the time of his arrival and I went up to join George who had already alerted the detective-sergeant who had booked in at the hotel and was botanising like fury within twenty-four hours.

George Waterston and I had to keep out of the way for fear of giving the game away and we used to meet the police officer once or twice a day at a pre-arranged spot not far from where the egg-collector was staying. Several days went by and although there was ample circum-stantial evidence to show that our quarry was after eggs, it had been impossible to pin him down. Then one morning when George and I were motoring to the rendezvous to meet the detective-sergeant the car broke down for a short period and we arrived nearly an hour late to find our friend hopping about from one foot to the other in a state of great agitation. It appeared that the collector was prematurely booking out and going back to England that very day. We dashed down to the nearest town to collect a couple of police constables and then came back to the hotel in the tiny village which did not boast a police station of its own. When the collector came out and was just about to drive away the detective-sergeant, who had been comparing wild flowers picked from the roadside with illustrations in a little pocket book, advanced upon him and the two police constables also dashed up.

The collector played the whole thing remarkably coolly and said, quite rightly, that the police had no powers to search his vehicle on the highway. He made the great mistake, however, of saying that he had

6

indeed collected some eggs but they were all of species which were not protected under the Act, e.g. pest species on the Second Schedule. He even went so far as to unearth a box which contained a number of gulls' eggs (which could be legally taken) and one clutch of oystercatchers. George Waterston, making one of the most brilliant errors he is ever likely to make in his life, said that the oystercatchers' eggs were protected. In fact this was not so, as in Scotland they had been included in the idiotic schoolboys' charter to which I have already referred. But the collector knew nothing about that Order, even though he appeared to know the Act from beginning to end; he was visibly shaken, and the detective-sergeant hung on grimly (though without ever going beyond what was right and proper) and eventually the collector capitulated and said that the car could be searched. The police officer was not to be drawn on this (he knew as well as anybody else that it would have been illegal to do so) and cleverly suggested that it would be easier if the collector got the boxes out himself in order to avoid any unnecessary disturbance.

He had a lot of eggs, some of them still unblown, including First Schedule species. He could have been fined many hundred pounds under the provision of the Act and certainly, allowing for time and costs involved, the effort to catch him must have cost a hundred or two. In the event he was fined £30 and so had the last laugh on everybody and there were two ironical sequels. In the next annual report of the Chief Constable it was stated that an offender had been successfully apprehended and prosecuted by his officers under the provisions of the Protection of Birds Act, without any acknowledgement being made to the efforts of the RSPB and a few years later the keeper who had assisted us in this episode and reaped his bonus, had himself to be prosecuted for the setting of illegal pole traps.

A patent, and indeed I would say a disastrous, weakness in the Protection of Birds Act lies in the fact that at present there are no powers for the police to search a person or a vehicle in a public place, even on grounds of reasonable suspicion that they have in fact committed an offence. I have always been in favour of the liberty of the subject, but one can carry this conception to ridiculous limits. There are, after all, very few innocent people who are likely to find themselves suspected by the police of possessing the eggs of birds illegally and if they were politely asked to reveal what they had in a bag over their shoulders or in the boot of their car, only the unreasonable would be likely to object. In any event, under the Game Act the police have had this power to search on grounds of reasonable suspicion that an offence has been committed and it is therefore absurd even for politicians to protest that something of the same kind should not be incorporated in the Protection of Birds Act, especially as it has become perfectly clear that unless this is done the police, who are presumably there to enforce the Acts which Parliament makes (otherwise why waste time and public money on making them?) must surely be given reasonable powers of enforcement; and the period since 1954 has also made it abundantly clear that the looting of rare birds' eggs can never be stopped unless this is done.

Although the osprey was one of the birds given special protection under the Act, the passage of which on to the statute book coincided almost exactly with its return to the highlands of Scotland after an absence of fifty years, the birds were almost certainly robbed of their eggs in both 1955 and 1956. It was not until the RSPB made a tremendous and costly effort to give them round-the-clock protection that they had any hope of succeeding at all and, even then, the nest was robbed under the very noses of the watchers in 1958. Although the intruder did not get away with his loot, the eggs were smashed in the process. Had he got away with the eggs and had it been possible to alert the police and perhaps find him just as he was reaching his car, as the Act stands at present there would have been nothing that could have been done, legally at any rate, except for everybody concerned to wish him the best of luck. Since then every year these massive guards have been mounted, though since the ospreys' nest has been open to the public, it could be argued that such organisation is necessary in order to exercise proper control. However, people do not go to look at ospreys in the middle of the night and anybody who has done a long watch from late evening to early morning, as I have done, is unlikely to be impressed by current legislation.

I realise as well as anybody else that the law in itself cannot necessarily give certain protection to any species. I realise also that the police have other, although not necessarily always more important, things to attend to. But if the Protection of Birds Act is really to be given effective teeth in suppressing the activities of nefarious collectors, two things are imperative. Firstly the police must be given similar powers of search to those given under the Game Acts. Secondly when there is a chance of really catching a collector redhanded, one or two plain-clothes men must be made available for the one or two days that may be necessary to catch the offender.

6 Conservation and Sport

For a considerable period it was generally considered that sport and conservation were opposing ideas. Granted that there were grounds for considering that this might well be so, developments in many countries have shown that, in practice, the two not only get on very well together but are mutually stimulating and interdependent.

No reasonable person would deny that shooting of any kind exerts some pressure upon a population of birds. But we know that the reproductive rate of almost all species is higher – often very much higher – than is necessary to sustain the population. Factors like starvation are, more often than not, the ultimate control.

The case of the wood pigeon in England is a good example. This common species is extremely beautiful, with a lovely, crooning song. It is also a great pest. In an exhaustive monograph, 'The Wood Pigeon' by R. K. Murton, it has been estimated that the cost of damage done by wood pigeons works out at about three to six shillings per head per annum. This may not sound very much but if we accept the figure then the total cost must be enormous. Furthermore, it is an average figure: pigeons in some areas do much more damage than in others. Apart from feeding voraciously on crops like clover, in cold winter weather they may descend in hordes upon green stuff, such as Brussels sprouts, and as much of the damage they do may be confined to a relatively short period of the year, a smallholder who may be unwillingly entertaining several hundred birds for weeks on end might well find that the damage finally runs into several hundred pounds. Under such circumstances, if you are grappling with a bank overdraft and a family of growing children, the aesthetic qualities of the wood pigeon are unlikely to deter you, or even to occur to you, as you reach for your gun. It is not always understood by townsmen who enjoy watching birds as a recreational pastime (a definition which would certainly cover the majority of members of organisations like the National Audubon Society of America and the RSPB in Britain) that many of them impinge in a very practical way, for good or ill, on the everyday working life of the countryman. So a jay stripping pea pods is just as beautiful as it is when eating acorns, but it is unlikely to please the owner of the peas.

Year in, year out, for decades the wood pigeons of England have been shot on a grand scale. Subsidies have been made available for the supply of cheap cartridges, pest-officers have laid on and advertised plans for special shoots and the pigeon has ridden roughshod over the lot. But it did not succeed, any more than any other creature will ever succeed, in riding roughshod over the laws of nature. Apart from the fact that there must always be an upper limit to any population, because of factors such as food-shortage leading to starvation or disease and, in some cases, limitation on the availability of suitable nesting-sites, severe winters can wreak havoc on many resident species in temperate zones. Along with a lot of other birds, wood pigeons suffered severely in Britain in the bitter and long winters of 1946–47 and 1962–63. In each case the reduction from peak numbers, which had apparently been maintained for many years after a rapid build-up from a previous 'low', was effected by a colossal death-rate due to simple starvation. In my part of the country one could pick up a score of corpses within a very few hundred yards, feather-light and emaciated to a degree which was almost unbelievable. The natural processes of nature can be, in one sense, brutal beyond the limits of almost the most vivid imagination. But mankind is in no position to cavil at this, for it is only by courtesy of these very processes that he has come into existence at all.

Although there are some 'highbrow' shots who will not stoop to it – more often than not, one suspects, because of their limitations as marksmen – the wood pigeon is a highly sporting bird. For this reason alone there will always be plenty of people to take some sort of an annual cull. If the Ministry of Agriculture are satisfied that a pigeon does, say, five shillings' worth of damage a year (and they ought to be, seeing that Dr Murton is one of their most able scientific advisers) then they might consider offering a bounty of four shillings for every pigeon shot, allowing the bird to be kept for sale. If a gunner only made a bob on the bird, it is certainly not difficult for an expert to account for anything up to 100 birds in a day, bad days of wind and weather being offset by others when the bag might be very much larger. Even allowing for the high cost of cartridges – the crack shot does not miss much – a man might earn anything from £25 to £50 a week by this means over a considerable part of the year.

It has sometimes been suggested that it was uncontrolled shooting which led to the extinction of the passenger pigeon in America. This idea now seems to be open to serious doubt. In *The World of Birds* James Fisher and Roger Tory Peterson state that the estimated total peak population in the first half of the nineteenth century was between three and five billion. It seems extremely unlikely that gunners could ever have accounted for more than the minutest fraction of such a population. Granted that they may well have had some effect in hastening the end when the passenger pigeon was on its last wings eighty or ninety years ago, I suggest that the root-cause for the loss of the species must lie elsewhere.

I am not, in this book, going to be drawn into ethical considerations of shooting for sport more often than I can help. I am, however, satisfied in my own mind that sport and conservation often do, and certainly can and should, progress in tandem; that, though ethical considerations have nothing to do with the conservationist *per se*, sport has more often than not, either directly or indirectly, been of immense benefit to the wild life of the world; and that any sportsmen worthy of the name is fully alive to the fact that his sport is doomed unless he can ensure the future survival of his quarry.

If the wood pigeon is well able to fend for itself, the same cannot be said of many other sporting birds. Duck and geese, for example, are experiencing a relatively rough time in the face of man's progress in many parts of the world. Development, for many wild creatures, is all too often synonymous with doom. But the conservationist has got to learn to live with progress, bending his efforts to try to modify it to his purposes whenever practicable. To this end it is fortunate, in both Britain and America, that wildfowlers and conservationists, the 'lunatic fringe' excepted, are working so well together.

There are, of course, still some parts of the world in which duck are flourishing in big numbers without any active assistance from man. I was recently talking to an Australian sportsman who had had some remarkable bags. On the other hand there are many areas where sporting quarry have been shot out of existence. A comparison between Italy and Great Britain, for instance, can surely leave no doubt in anybody's mind that a proper policy of game preservation and wild life management is absolutely essential. I suppose there is no such thing as a real standard in sport, by which I mean that one cannot lay down rules and notions as if they were facts. Yet how surprised an Englishman or an American would be if in his own country he found a tethered owl set up as a decoy with gunners sitting behind bushes and waiting to pot at migrating barn-swallows coming in to mob the decoy bird. I think it is true to say that the typical sporting shot in Britain (and I think this applies in America too) regards two sorts of quarry as reasonable: those that can be utilised as food and those which are pests. Of course many small birds are in fact edible, but from a sporting angle, it really does seem a little ludicrous that they should be regarded as worthy of powder and shot, and many people would dispute the idea that the majority of them are obtained in a sporting manner. But the fact of the matter is that there are many countries where for several reasons there are very few worthwhile birds left to shoot. There may be many people who dislike the principle of private ownership of land, but from the point of view of the conservationist it has been and still is a tremendous asset in the preservation of most wild life outside specific reservations.

It is relevant here to consider the situation in the two Maltese islands of Malta and Gozo. These together cover an area about the size of the

Isle of Wight and they are jam-packed with a population of 330,000, and one which is steadily rising in spite of considerable emigration. Although they may not all have gun licences, it has been estimated, I suspect pretty accurately, that something like 70,000 Maltese possess and use guns. Apart from a few warblers and small birds of that kind, practically no birds are protected. Innumerable finches and other small birds are trapped on migration and traded as cage birds, of which the Maltese are extremely fond, but almost anything as large as a quail is relentlessly pursued by the gunners. When I was there in the spring of 1963 I had one or two glimpses of a wood sandpiper on the west side of Malta. This was one of the shyest birds I have ever seen – and no wonder. Half a dozen people seemed to be always watching with guns in an attempt to shoot it and it may well have been the only wading bird in an area of two or three square miles. One Sunday when visiting the only fresh-water lake which is surrounded by a small marsh, the owner came along and skilfully beat it with an excellent dog, finally putting up the only snipe which could have been there. He missed with both barrels and I cannot say I was sorry. All this in the middle of March on a marsh where even the most elementary standards of preservation would at least ensure that a few birds of some kind or another would nest. There is certainly no reason why quail should not regularly breed in Malta, but the sportsmen never even allow them a chance to settle down before killing and eating them, though a few are trapped and kept alive as decoy birds. Those that are killed are the lucky ones, for these decoys have to live in tiny little hutches in which they usually have to stand or sit lengthwise and can quite obviously only turn round with difficulty. The Maltese are not unkind and I doubt if it ever occurs to most of them that these quail are almost certainly at least uncomfortable if not unhappy. Whilst efforts are being made in north-west Europe to preserve marsh and Montagu's harriers, the Maltese cheerfully shoot them when they are on migration and so far as I can see they shoot almost anything that flies except perhaps during the great season of the turtle dove passage.

The spring migration of the turtle dove is the highlight of the Maltese sporting season, though it usually only lasts for ten days or a fortnight around the end of April and the beginning of May. The moment the first turtle doves are spotted on the island on their northward passage the word is flashed round on the bush telegraph and everybody who possibly can spends most of his time in the next ten days or so shooting at doves. The numbers of the birds are variable, but I believe it has been estimated, pretty reliably, I think, that as many as 20,000 may be shot in a fortnight. Mass is said on Sundays at half-past two in the morning in order that the shooters can be out and about as soon as it gets light. There are so many guns about that it is a miracle that more people do not get shot. Very often one dove is shot almost simultaneously by two or three gunners and it is usually the unwritten rule, so I understand, that it then belongs to the person who retrieves it first, either personally or via his dog if he has one. Let it be understood that the birds are almost invariably eaten and that they are in many ways as sporting a target as wood pigeons or partridges. But, although it may be argued that the turtle dove is still a pretty common species in areas where it nests in northern Europe and that 20,000 kills in Malta must make little difference to the total numbers, it surely runs against all the best principles of wild life management to destroy a sporting bird just before it is about to breed.

I have no doubt that the Maltese would counter this by saying that, apart from this one fortnight with the doves, there is practically no worthwhile shooting throughout the rest of the year, but one answer to that is that not the slightest attempt appears to be made to get some policy of proper management, by the introduction of close seasons and so on. I am sure that the difficulties are immense just as they would be in southern Italy where the situation is not dissimilar. But surely it is the difficulties which provide the challenges in modern life and save us all from boredom?

To turn from the specific to the general, there are a number of ways in which some limitations can be placed upon the numbers of sporting birds which may be shot. Perhaps the most obvious one is by way of a bag limit as widely practised in North America and Australia. Here one has a permit, for which one often has to pay quite heavily, which broadly speaking entitles one to shoot so many birds of such and such species. British wildfowlers may be startled to learn that it may cost them anything up to a couple of pounds sterling to shoot a mallard or a goose in the United States. On the other hand the State or the Federal Government does make use of that money in providing refuges for wildfowl, which is more than can be said in favour of the governments of a good many other countries, who are all too apt to take licence fees as by divine right and use them for purposes not even remotely connected with sport or conservation. There are, however, certain drawbacks to the bag limit idea. Provided that you have the money and two or three friends who would like a non-shooting outing, you may be able to get four permits and shoot, so to speak, four bags full. This trick is certainly practised in Australia.

In most western European countries, including Britain, bag limits do not apply. On the whole it is left to the good sense of the individual and the system works very well, but it is always desirable firstly to have a close season which is really long enough to cover the whole of the breeding season, and secondly to make it possible to shorten or even for a period completely stop the open season, if there is a serious decline in the numbers of a particular species. Thus, the brent goose has been fully protected in Great Britain since 1954 and is now also protected in most other countries in north-western Europe, and it seems evident that the species has profited by a small but significant increase in numbers following a long period of decline to a fairly low ebb. Ten years ago when anxiety was felt over the wintering stocks of barnacle geese in Britain, that species too was fully protected, and again there was an increase in numbers so that now they can be shot in a limited part of their wintering range for a short season of two months.

Within living memory the shooting season for wildfowl in Britain ran from August 1st until the following March. It still does so in a number of important European countries, such as France. There are very good reasons behind the present British season which runs from September 1st to January 31st, a period of five months only, plus a special dispensation for an extra three weeks for migratory duck on the foreshore. In some areas many mallard, even if they do not actually lay eggs in February (and some do), ought not to be unnecessarily disturbed at that time, whilst at the beginning of August many of the young from late broods are still 'flappers'.

There are plenty of people who can write with much more authority on game and wildfowl management than the present writer. However, one thing should be stressed and that is that any efforts which may be taken to sustain a species in the winter time will be doomed to failure if its breeding haunts are becoming steadily more restricted and more disturbed. There is at the present time in Britain a body of opinion which feels that the season for partridge shooting which runs from September 1st to February 1st and which has been unchanged for generations, should be curtailed. That the partridge has for many years been in a serious state of decline is beyond dispute. In some areas it is now almost extinct and only in a few places, mostly where birds are reared on a massive scale, is it present in anything like its former numbers. One must avoid being too dogmatic about the reasons for this alarming drop in the numbers of partridges, but there is no reason to suppose that it is not connected to a large extent with the demands of modern agriculture. Compared with even thirty years ago, there is now relatively little cover in which a partridge can make a nest and lay its eggs well screened from crows and other predators and with adequate shelter from inclement weather. Even when it does do so, some mechanical contraption may well come along and destroy all its chances of reproducing its kind. Anyway, if we assume that this is a basic reason for the decline, then no amount of juggling about with close seasons is likely to make any significant difference.

As most readers will know, the majority of game birds receive a good deal of preferential treatment and in view of the good sport and the good eating which they provide, nobody should grudge them this. But were it not for this and rearing on a large scale, the pheasant would almost certainly be a relatively uncommon British bird. Now the wildfowlers are also making serious and worthwhile attempts to rear mallard on a fair scale, and they are also experimenting with other species. This movement is gaining momentum. At the moment the annual output of duck reared and released is rather over 11,000. Furthermore this scheme is undertaken by local wildfowling clubs or individuals and it is certainly a most practical and worthwhile way of making wildfowlers conservation-minded should they not already have seen the light. In addition the Wildfowlers' Association of Great Britain and Ireland (WAGBI) have in recent years, under special licence from the Nature Conservancy, been reintroducing into England greylag-geese from their very limited breeding grounds in Scotland. This scheme has met with considerable initial success, the offspring of the geese having been released on reserves where they have already bred more than one generation of their own. It should be borne in mind that these birds are truly wild stock. I doubt myself if anything has been more imaginative and its educational value seems to me to be much greater than most of the ideas protectionists have hitherto thought up. For example, most of these greylag are now breeding in a part of the Lake District and fly out in winter over a coastal marsh which is leased by one of the prominent local clubs. In winter, of course, there are other geese, too, and there is no need for me to stress how eager some of the younger members of that club must be to shoot their first goose. Yet simply because there would be a risk of shooting one of the greylag, nobody at the present moment shoots any geese at all, even though it would be perfectly legitimate for them to do so.

Strangely enough there are signs that some conservationists do not look at all favourably either upon the scheme for rearing mallard or on the reintroduction of the wild greylag into England. So far as it is possible to understand these objections, it seems that these schemes are regarded as artificial, i.e. unnatural but, quite apart from the fact that the general urgency demands that conservation should not be treated as if it were a game of checkers, the whole concept of conservation in many countries has become highly artificial in any case. Not only have habitats been altered beyond all recognition, but almost every well-run reserve is a continuous battle to prevent natural forces getting the upper hand. Quite apart from the fact that something like twenty per cent of the British flora is now entirely alien, we have destroyed huge areas of natural heathlands and planted them up with coniferous trees which are in any purist view synthetic. If there had been a land bridge between East Anglia and the Netherlands, it is highly probable that many of the extensive and highly artificial coniferous forests in Norfolk and Suffolk would by now have contained crested tits. Nor is there any reason to suppose that if this species were intentionally introduced they could possibly cause any harm. I stress this because in principle I think one must always be extremely cautious in one's advocacy of bringing in any creatures from another region. But reintroduction of species which have disappeared or introduction of a race of the same species (and there is another resident race of crested tits in the north of Scotland) seems to carry no real element of risk, quite apart from the fact that people would obtain interest and pleasure from seeing a bird like the crested tit in East Anglia. In what is from the point of view of wild life a rapidly shrinking world, it seems essential that every effort should be made to make the maximum possible use of what is left.

I do not want to hurt anybody's feelings but in a period when it is generally admitted that the wild life of the world is in peril, that urgent action is essential if we are to save a considerable part of it, it is imperative that we should breed practical conservationists rather than playboys.

7 Introductions and Re-introductions

Introductions and re-introductions raise such important and controversial issues as to justify discussion at somewhat greater length. As escaped exotics, like the mink and the coypu, have caused considerable damage and alarm it cannot be too strongly emphasised that, unless the greatest care is taken, the results may be disastrous, not only to man's own interests but to those of many other animals, including those most in need of care and protection.

Many people are surprised to learn that species like the rabbit and the pheasant are not indigenous. But most naturalists have long accepted the first as, so to speak, a naturalised alien and the population of the rabbit has been knocked sideways since the advent of that hideous and nauseating example of biological control of a pest, myxomatosis. Economically, I suppose, it is quite impossible to enter any plea in favour of the rabbit, but, apart from the fact that it gave many of us some good sport and fun with a gun (and will survive to do so) its sudden and swift decline completely upset a balance which had been developed over a very long period, certainly detrimental to the welfare of some birds, the uncommon stone curlew to take one example.

But there are a number of birds now living and breeding successfully in either a completely wild or semi-feral state. The gadwall, a duck which *may* have spread naturally into Scotland but which was certainly introduced into England; the delightful mandarin, which breeds freely in a few localities and which is alleged by some to be commoner now in Britain than in its native China; the Carolina duck from America, which is at present nesting free on a tiny scale and confined, I believe, to one or two localities in the midlands; the red-legged partridge from Hungary; the little owl from the Netherlands and the Canada goose from America.

Very few of these introductions have been a nuisance. Granted that the phenomenal spread of the little owl since about the end of the nineteenth century has not been universally welcomed. Those responsible for game-preservation thought it was something of a disaster. This was to some extent countered by an inquiry organised by the British Trust for Ornithology just prior to the Second World War, which certainly showed that many of the charges had been grossly exaggerated. In those days when the majority (not all) of sportsmen and protectionists ranged themselves up on opposite sides and carried on a sort of form of unarmed combat, the protectionists greeted the results of that inquiry with great glee. Many sportsmen, fortified to some degree by the evidence of their own eyes and the reports of their game-keepers – not all of which were greatly exaggerated – rather stupidly appeared to believe that the little owl had no virtues. They even produced some of the cruel and glaring eyes twaddle, closely related to the mawkish sentimentality of many of the earlier and a few of the latter-day protectionists. But when the little owl turned up on one or two bird-reserves and began attacking species like the storm petrel, some of its supporters rather sharply changed their tune. Sauce for the goose being sauce also for the gander, one might be justified in suggesting that no action should be taken against the little owl under such circumstances until at least there is some evidence to show that this delightfully charming but relatively common little sea-bird is being taken in sufficient numbers to have at least some slight effect on the overall population. Possibly those in charge of a local reserve would counter this by saying that what they were concerned with was not the total population of petrels but the numbers which patronised their particular little niche. This is precisely the attitude taken by the average gamekeeper: he is

The British Parliament banned the use of the pole-trap in 1904. Sixty years later it is still in use. This one, rusty and disused, was found set in the eyrie of a golden eagle.

An illegal pole-trap set near the nest of a peregrine, which is itself a protected bird in so far as the law has any effective say in the matter.

A black-tailed godwit, this bird is now nesting in Britain once more after being extinct as a breeding species for twenty years.

A hen harrier shot in Ireland and displayed for the local paper under the headline 'Eagle shot in Cork'; the proud hunter claimed that this was the third 'eagle' he had shot!

not concerned about the total number of game chicks which may be taken by little owls over the country as a whole : it is what happens on his beat which is important to him.

I cannot see that the introductions of these birds, nor the re-introduction of a species like the capercaillie, have done any great harm. The little owl, at least, might ultimately have arrived under its own steam. And what are we likely to say about the collared dove? This pretty, but non-migratory relative of the familiar turtle dove has exploded from Asia Minor and Turkey all over north-west Europe within the last hundred years, with rapidly increasing momentum in the last twenty or thirty. It reached England just over ten years ago, was promptly put on the list of specially protected birds (and, let me confess, I was one of the people who helped to put it there, though its continued spread would never have been halted, protected bird or not). Now it is established in quite a big way, from Kent to the Outer Hebrides and from Cornwall to the Shetlands and there is no reason to suppose that it will not continue to increase, becoming something more than a minor nuisance in the process, maybe. But the point that may be made is that this was not a deliberate introduction of an alien bird : it came in naturally, not artificially. The purist, no doubt, will accept it without demur.

Yet, in the strict sense of the word, has the collared dove really spread naturally to Britain? It is a bird which seems to be almost as dependent upon the activities of man as does the house sparrow, feeding largely on grain in and around suitable poultry runs and farmsteads and presumably for this reason, as in Holland and elsewhere, it has a curiously patchy distribution, quite large concentrations being separated by miles where not a single pair are to be seen. Could this explosion have occurred even two or three centuries ago? Of course, nobody can answer that question but it is worth pondering. The whole order of things has become so highly artificial that I doubt whether the purist, in spite of his scientific integrity, has really got much of a leg to stand on. And, because it is the variety rather than the mere numbers of birds which is valued so much by most people, he needs a very good case indeed.

7

It must also be realised that many of the birds that we have got get highly artificial treatment. Bird reserves belong to the next chapter; but it is relevant to mention here that they are highly artificial. It is not only a question of 'farming' the habitat for the express purpose of impeding the natural sequence of events. Some animals are deliberately destroyed in order that others may thrive the better. Feeding birds in winter (or at any other season) is another highly artificial form of 'interference' which is increasing in Great Britain and North America. If it assists any species at all, it obviously does so most to those which are more adaptable and probably best able to look after themselves, anyway. It is even possible, if not probable, that it does no good to conservation at all, because the feeding is often intermittent. Having attracted an unusually large number of birds into a big garden, what is likely to happen when the benevolent owners go off for a fortnight's holiday at Christmas and the weather turns sour? Reverting to nest boxes, most people seem to be very happy that the pied flycatcher has been induced to extend its range by providing it with breeding sites. I am happy, too, for the more we can see of this attractive bird the better. But the whole conception is artificial. The RSPB put up a number of Scandinavian type nest boxes in the hope that wintering goldeneye in the Highlands of Scotland might thus be induced to stay and breed. Apart from the fact that I have a hunch that any pair of goldeneye so-minded would have little difficulty in finding a suitable home of their own, surely these are the kind of enterprises which are to be highly commended.

The contrary argument would presumably run along the lines that, if the goldeneye did use an artificial box, then they had every intention of staying to breed and the nest box was purely coincidental with this urge. And the pied flycatchers, although they had extended their range by using nest boxes without which that extension would not have occurred, had migrated to Britain, they were British breeding stock and they would have at least tried to breed.

What is so sacrosanct about Britain in this respect, anyway? National boundaries are usually mere man-made conceptions. Some of the ancestors of swallows which might now be described as Russian (because they breed in Russia) were Polish (because they once bred in Poland). The boundaries of states, like the divisions which exist within them, may have their uses for what one might call the convenient pigeon-holing of records but they are purely man-made, liable to alteration without notice and more often than not they are unrelated to any natural boundaries between one type of scenery or habitat and another.

I must leave readers to think about it and form their own ideas. But I think it does need thought. I would again say that I am not, in this particular period of time, anyway, in favour of deliberately introducing exotic species. Nor do I feel that the subject should be tackled on any wholesale scale. The introducion of the continental race of the crested tit into East Anglia is a perfectly good example of what I would have in mind. The habitat for the bird has already almost certainly been made, and made artificially. Similar afforestation schemes only a few hundred miles away in the Netherlands have shown that the crested tit will spread into them naturally. The North Sea may well be the only barrier which prevents us not only enjoying watching one of the loveliest birds in an attractive family, but actually increasing the European stock of a bird which is not particularly common as small birds go and which is rare indeed in Great Britain at the present time.

As conservationists we are all rightly alarmed at the way in which habitats for wild life are diminishing rapidly all over the world. We cry out that today we must all make every effort to do all that we can to save what is left of the wild life of the world, for tomorrow will be too late. We must strive to hand on to generations to come what we have inherited and enjoyed and held in trust. There is no doubt that the wilderness is in retreat but what sort of a charge will lie against us if future generations discover that, though we had the knowledge and skill, we yet failed to try to ensure that every new habitat which we had created was not filled with the maximum variety of wild life.

8 Bird Reserves – Some Problems and Experiments

Earlier in this book reference was made to the embryonic growth of bird sanctuaries or bird reserves. Even if some of these earlier attempts were sometimes of little or no importance the concept was a good one. However, even fifty or sixty years ago, it was probably impossible to foresee the colossal pressures that would be put upon wild life as the wilderness receded. Perhaps the most staggering changes are occurring in the newly emergent countries, especially in Africa. There is no getting away from the fact that to a very large extent human progress is disastrous to animals. It seems almost certain that the next few decades, or at any rate the next century, will see a further opening up and development of not only jungle areas in the tropics but perhaps also of the Arctic and Antarctic regions, which have hitherto belonged to those tough creatures, by no means few in number, which have had them to themselves.

Some of these wider issues will be dealt with in the next chapter. In dealing here specifically with reserves, I think there are one or two points which ought to be made clear from the outset. At any rate until after the Second World War, a genuine wild life reserve was almost unknown in Britain, although in fact, thanks to a very great extent to sporting interests and the fact that large estates were under private ownership, very considerable areas were truly reservations in all but name. True, they were not developed or exploited on the broadest possible lines, and even rarer birds of prey were as likely as not to be destroyed simply on an outdated principle that all birds with hooked beaks were incompatible with game preservation.

I have dealt with birds of prey at some length in a previous volume in this series (*Birds of Prey*: Survival Books, No. 1). It is therefore unnecessary to go into specific details now, though it is as well to point out that on all the evidence available at the moment, it is very often necessary to exercise some measure of control in a reserve.

Small countries like Britain and the Netherlands have not got the space which is available in the vast areas of Canada and the United States or Australia – just to take a few examples. It is probably a fair generalisation to say that the larger a reserve may be, the less management per acre, so to speak, will be necessary. However, the fact that management is important has been shown very clearly in a book by Colin Willock, *The Enormous Zoo*, which deals with two National wild life parks in Uganda, the Queen Elizabeth and the Murchison Falls. In one of these there are enormous numbers of hippos, all with enormous appetites and requiring anything up to a ton to a ton and a half of herbage a week to nourish their enormous bulk. They were therefore in great competition with other smaller herbivores. Apart from actually eating the grass the hippos rolled and wallowed about in it, destroying a great deal of valuable food in the process. As soon as the situation had been worked out, it was decided to take an annual cull of hippos in order to bring their numbers down and to maintain them at a level which would give some of their weaker competitors for the food supply a fair chance. Highly artificial, of course, but, as I have said more than once before, in a world which we have made largely synthetic, we can no longer expect to have it otherwise.

In even small bird reserves, problems of much the same kind arise. One of the old established RSPB reserves covers part of the remarkable shingle beach at Dungeness in Kent. This enormous area of shingle, which has no parallel in all Europe, was built over centuries by the scouring action of strong sea currents throwing up millions of tons of stones from the sea bed to form a huge rampart on the south-east side of Romney Marsh. Here there was, at the beginning of the twentieth century, a large and flourishing colony of terns as well as a good number of gulls and other species. The area was wardened and as the habitat was one which was not subject to any significant annual changes, the birds flourished. Then came Hitler's war and the whole area was requisitioned by the War Department and used as a bombing and firing range. It is doubtful whether this in itself was particularly detrimental to the birds because animals, generally speaking, get very used to noise and movement, provided that it does not do them physical injury. Most of the nesting colonies happened to be in the safety area beyond the firing range. But the trouble was that at weekends and other times when firing was not taking place, the local people raided the gull and tern colonies in order to utilise their eggs – an operation which was at least very understandable at a time when the nation's larder was at a low ebb and the diet, if healthy, extremely monotonous.

It was not until around 1950 that the War Department finally relinquished the area which had been requisitioned from the RSPB, though I am bound to doubt whether there is any living Brass Hat who could advance any reason whatsoever why this action could not have been taken much earlier. If there is an acid edge on this remark, I can perhaps best explain it by saying that the Service departments have been singularly greedy, not only in seizing but in hanging on to areas of the utmost importance to wild life. One cannot help feeling that often ranges could have been shared between the various Services and in any event there are times when many of them have been used very little if at all. However, to return to Dungeness, once the land came back to it the RSPB appointed a warden with a view to trying to re-establish the remnants of a herring gull colony which then numbered rather less than 100 pairs. So far as one now knows, herring gulls and terns are not perhaps the best neighbours, though here again we are faced with the sort of problem where it may well be much better to try to strike some reasonable balance than to exterminate completely a larger and predatory species. However, in spite of protection, the herring gulls declined quickly. They reared practically no young, partly because eggs were taken by carrion crows, which had become very numerous during the period when the War Department were in control and partly due to other causes such as foxes taking young chicks. It also seems likely that simply because their eggs had been taken for many years, most of the adult herring gulls were rather aged. Anyway the colony declined until it virtually disappeared.

Terns migrated along the coast regularly each spring, but they belonged to established colonies elsewhere and only a very few attempted to breed, and no proper colony has ever been established since. Apart from foxes, research by the warden showed that hedgehogs preyed heavily on the eggs of terns and other birds, even though these curious prickly urchins must have had to travel many hundreds of yards on their nightly prowls. Subsequent developments have been very different from what could have been foreseen in 1950. In the first place the whole character of a unique and genuinely wild area – one of the few truly wild places which was still left in the whole of the south of England – was selected as a site for a nuclear power station. Tremendous battles waged between on the one hand the Central Electricity Generating Board and the government minister responsible for fuel and power, and on the other the conservation interests led by the Nature Conservancy. It was touch and go, but in the end the power station won and one more irreplaceable bit of scenery was ruined aesthetically. However, most wild animals are not, so far as we know, concerned with man's conception of what is or is not beautiful. Dungeness did not come to a stop and indeed at the present time plans are well ahead, thanks to extensive gravel excavation, for the area to rank high in the future as a water-bird reserve. Perhaps even more relevant is that this development is a joint venture between the conservationists and the wildfowlers, if, for the sake of convenience, I may be allowed to split them.

A different example of the problems that arise has occurred at Havergate Island in Suffolk. As already related, avocets returned to breed here shortly after the war on a small portion of the area enclosed by the sea walls which had been flooded by salt water because of accidental damage to the sluice. In order to make more ground available for these birds, special sluices were put in so that large lagoons could be flooded with salt water and the level strictly controlled so that the low mud islets on which the avocets built their nests were not flooded in the event of heavy and prolonged rain. The avocets settled in well but so had a sizeable colony of black-headed gulls which found conditions to their liking. From 1948 until about 1954 gulls and avocets both increased in very roughly the same proportions, the gulls from two or three hundred pairs to two or three thousand, and the avocets from half a dozen pairs to nearly 100. Then, whilst each year the gulls maintained or even increased in numbers, the avocets started to decline. Many pairs lost their eggs and many chicks perished. Gulls were actually seen killing small avocet chicks. Some chicks, however, were picked up in an emaciated condition and may have died from starvation, and as a high proportion of recent summers have been abnormally wet and cold in June, there may well be other factors besides gull predation which adversely affects the chicks of the avocets. However, the enormous increase in the size of the gull colony, coupled with the admittedly largely circumstantial evidence that they were competing with and even killing some of the young avocets, led to the adoption of control measures. The black-headed gull, though an attractive bird, is very common in Britain and there was therefore no reasonable objection to experimenting in this way by trying to reduce their population on the island.

It is, of course, one thing to talk about control and another thing to put it into practice. During all the years when the avocet population had been increasing it had been a rule that only on the rarest occasions did the warden or anybody else go out among the nesting birds. The most obvious way to check the reproduction rate of the gulls seemed to be to destroy their eggs and this was done by pricking a percentage of them systematically each year. There was, however, for the first time some disturbance of the avocets and great care had to be exercised during the operation. At first there was no apparent effect and year by year the number of eggs which were destroyed was stepped up until it reached eighty or ninety per cent. Now in the mid-sixties, the black-headed gulls have been reduced to less than one hundred pairs and the avocet population has remained more or less stable for several years at between fifty and sixty pairs. The original intention was that the gulls would not be exterminated and, as the avocets flourished so well during the period when there were less than a thousand gulls, there would appear to be something to be said for such a policy. Once you have a species under control, it is probably not very difficult to keep the population within narrow limits. I understand, however, that the RSPB has now changed its original policy and intends to wipe out the black-headed gulls completely from Havergate Island. It must seem to some people, including myself, a pity that the experiment was not tried of seeing what happens if a small colony of gulls were allowed to remain, particularly as the avocets are no longer declining. Apart from the fact that it would not be very difficult to put the pressure on a small number of gulls at almost any moment, this is the sort of opportunity which the conservationist in these days cannot afford to miss. Because of lack of knowledge he must sometimes work by empirical rules and accept circumstantial evidence, if and when he is unable to get at the true facts, but if the gulls are completely driven away and the avocets remain at their present population, which is about two-thirds of the maximum reached when the gulls were very common, it will leave the basic puzzle completely unresolved.

In many ways the examples given of protection at Dungeness and of the avocets on Havergate Island are relatively simple, even if the problems, let alone the solutions, are by no means properly understood. In many bird reserves conditions are infinitely more complicated. An example of this can be found only a few miles north of Havergate on the bird reserve at Minsmere. This is 1,500 acres in extent, which is really ridiculously small. Yet as pure bird reserves go, it is one of the biggest in England. Here one of the most important birds is the very rare bearded tit. It is a tiny and utterly charming bird, which is nearly all tail, and which lives in the dense reeds. In 1947, following a prolonged and bitter winter, it is believed that there may have been only a handful of birds left in the whole of East Anglia, indeed not more than one or two pairs nested at Minsmere where at that time, owing to the salt flooding, the reed beds were nothing like as extensive or thick as they are today. At Hickling in Norfolk, the only other locality where they were known to be present in the spring of 1947, only a single cock bird was seen, though of course the odd bird or two could have been overlooked.

What is a fact is that the bearded tit came as near as possible at that time to ceasing to be a British breeding species. Fortunately the hens lay four or five eggs in well-concealed nests amongst dense reeds and as the breeding season is a long one, extending in most years from mid-April until well on into July, two or even three broods may be reared by a single pair in a favourable summer. In other words, like the majority of small passerine birds, the bearded tit has remarkable powers of re-covery. It has since increased greatly and although it has had one or two severe setbacks, notably in the cold winter of 1962–63, it is now breeding outside its traditional coastal strongholds in the counties of Norfolk and Suffolk. It is interesting that it appears to hold on best in suitable marshes like Minsmere, immediately adjacent to the North Sea. This may well be related to the fact that in a bitter winter, when it suffers most, cold easterly winds coming off the North Sea tend to be slightly warmer than they would be even a very few miles inland. Certainly through favourable periods the birds increase and appear to spread away to marshes some distance from the coast in the Broads and elsewhere and it may well be that it is the proximity of the sea which enables coastal birds to survive hard winters better than the others. However, there does seem to be little doubt that in spite of all the efforts which have been made, with considerable success, to build up the numbers of these tits, a really prolonged and hard winter might exter-minate them utterly.

It is just these possibilities that the conservationist must face, nor are they in any way confined to one species like the bearded tit; there are others like the rare Dartford warbler which barely holds on in some of the heathlands in southern England when the weather is bitterly cold. One may be disturbed at the remarkable and very visible decline of many of the commoner birds such as thrushes and wrens following a severe winter, but in fact these birds are so relatively common that it is, generally speaking, only a matter of a very few seasons before the numbers return to normal. But when we come to rarities like the Dartford warbler and the bearded tit, the populations, even following a sequence of milder winters, may well be reckoned only in hundreds or at best a thousand or two, and the safety margin is very slight indeed.

Obviously nothing can be done to ameliorate the climate of any area but on the assumption that it is desirable to maintain species on the limits of their range (though there are some people who will suggest, on fairly sensible grounds, that it might be better to take a more international view and to use available resources to preserve essential habitats in the areas where the birds are more firmly established) then some thought must be given as to how one might be able to get a vulnerable species like the bearded tit through a bad winter. One possible solution, which I believe should be looked at very seriously, is to consider whether it might not be possible to secure a small number of birds in the late autumn and to keep them in captivity for release in the following spring. At the end of a good summer there may be several hundred bearded tits on the Minsmere marsh and in October many of these migrate and go off to winter elsewhere, perhaps not to return in the spring. If ten or twenty birds could be captured and looked after during the winter and released in the spring, even if through some misfortune something like half of them died, enough would remain to form the nucleus of a new breeding stock, even if all the birds which were free were killed in a severe winter. Of course this sort of thing would require experiment and it might prove quite impracticable in some cases to keep the birds alive at all. The advice of skilled aviculturists would have to be sought and some might argue that it would be better, if the birds were wiped out, to try to re-introduce a number of them from abroad. However, apart from the fact that some of the purists might be against this sort of thing (not that I have any patience with them) it might also be found that birds from abroad, which have been for generations used to much more amenable winters, would not survive the English climate, even in the average winter, nearly as well as our own well-conditioned stock.

Whilst on the subject of Minsmere, the opportunity can be taken for mentioning again the difficulties which beset those responsible for the running of effective reserves in maintaining something approaching the *status quo* in the habitats. In the early 1950's two birds which have almost disappeared from Minsmere, one very uncommon and the other relatively so, the stone curlew and the woodlark, were comparatively common. The stone curlews nested on the heathland at a density well above one pair per hundred acres. The heather had been knocked about and large open areas created when the area had been used during the Second World War as a tank training ground. Even when the tanks had at last departed, the rabbits, which were very numerous, helped to keep the new growth in check, but the heather slowly began to re-establish itself together with a considerable growth of young birch and some coarse grasses. When in the mid-fifties myxomatosis almost annihilated the rabbit population overnight, the stone curlews very soon found that their nesting grounds became quite unsuitable for breeding.

Attempts were made to counteract this situation by hiring a bull-dozer to take off the top surface of heather in certain areas, but this, in spite of being very expensive, did not prove satisfactory, so that now the stone curlew is a rare bird indeed at Minsmere and in most years only one or two pairs attempt to breed. It should be noted that this has happened in spite of the fact that the area is a private reserve and is adequately wardened and kept free from undue public disturbance.

The woodlark, of which there used to be a number of pairs, has also become rare or non-existent at Minsmere, because once the rabbit disappeared the short herbage which was suitable to the bird soon grew up into a tangle of rank grass.

Much of the work that needs to be done urgently in reserve management is of a scientific nature. There is already a good deal of literature extant on the subject and all I would like to do is to emphasize that important as it is, scientific management is not everything. Essential prerequisites to a well-run reserve are adequate wardening, which means in effect that a man is required who is both knowledgeable, tactful and firm, and it is a mistake in these days to think that such people can be got on the cheap. Secondly, in most cases anyway, it is imperative to have the goodwill of all the local inhabitants in the neighbourhood of the reserve. This goodwill can be fostered in a number of ways, really too simple to require further elucidation here. It is a good rule never to try to talk above the level of the local people, who may well be highly intelligent, but few of whom will be ornithologists. One of the most embarrassing evenings of my life, though fortunately I was only a neutral onlooker, was at a meeting where two scientists were trying to explain why a nature reserve had been declared in a certain area from which the public were to be more or less excluded. Something approaching 100 local people sat with long faces whilst a learned gentleman (and he was learned) spoke at length about such matters as the zonation of plant life and ecological successions. At length one member of the audience got up and interrupted and asked for explanations, and suggested, I thought rightly, that if the speaker was talking about the way in which wild plants colonised an area which was being built up into the sea, why could he not use the sort of language that the common man could understand. It may be a bit of an exaggeration, but I believe that the unfortunate scientist had perhaps almost forgotten how to explain things in lay language.

An obvious difficulty in all wild life reserves, bird or otherwise, is to know how to cater for members of the public. It has always seemed to me that a responsibility rests upon those who run these reserves to make sure that the animals and plants inside them can be seen by people. Granted that they may be of great importance as open air scientific laboratories, this should never be allowed to be used in itself as an excuse for not letting as many people into them as is reasonably possible, provided the people want to come. Almost all the private reservations are maintained by the subscriptions of ordinary people like you and me and even state-owned reserves get the funds for their maintenance out of the tax-payer's pocket. Nine times out of ten it is perfectly simple to allow public access on quite a large scale along recognised routes and preferably with suitable hides provided. It is not so much the numbers of people who may come along, but the control of them once they are there. Birds, at any rate, get extremely used to people if they regularly appear at a certain spot. It is movement in a strange place, or in many cases near to their nests, which is damaging. On some quite large reserves visitors are limited to perhaps fifteen or twenty people a day, when in fact, provided some system can be devised so that they do not all arrive and move around together, it would often be feasible to handle five or ten times that number.

One excellent example of what I mean is in the United States where at the Brigantine Wild Life Reserve in New Jersey, after reporting to the warden, there is no restriction upon any number of people driving their cars along a number of routes from which splendid views of many birds can be obtained.

There is perhaps no need to point out that bird reserves have their limitations. The majority of rare birds in Britain, for instance – and this probably goes for most other countries as well – nest outside reserves; probably all the kites in Wales do so, as do also the ospreys in Scotland, though under a dispensation in the Protection of Birds Act the famous pair at Loch Garten are breeding in what is nominally a sanctuary. But what is so striking about the ospreys is that although to-day they are Britain's rarest birds, the Loch Garten pair are being viewed by something over 20,000 people each year during the three months or so of the breeding season. This is approximately the number of persons who may be allowed on to a bird reserve like Minsmere during the next twenty years or so.

9 Birds in the Balance

The writer does not claim that this book is anything more than an introduction to bird conservation and some of the many problems which concern and often baffle the conservationist. The limitations of our knowledge are at present so great that very often we are like the proverbial doctor who, having tried one course of treatment upon a patient and finding it has no visible effect for the better, promptly changes the prescription and sits back to see which way the pendulum swings. Any genuine effort to preserve the natural scene, even if it fails, is not to be sneered at in a century when so much is being lost so quickly. At the same time there is, I believe, a danger that many of us are failing to see the wood for the trees. Excluding special cases like the desperate fight to save the Californian condor in California (which ought to be a world priority), or the all-out efforts to re-establish the osprey as a breeding bird in Scotland (which is tremendously exciting and by no means unimportant, but which if it had not been for the ghastly threat posed by the use of poisonous pesticides would be of much more local importance than the case of the condor) – excluding these cases which admittedly are legion, the struggle for conservation is never going to revolve round such relatively trivial things as boys taking the eggs of hedge-nesting birds, or in feeding birds in suburban gardens and things of that kind. I would not say that these things have no importance but in the long run any effect they are likely to have is going to be completely masked by other changes. Even bird reserves have their limitations, not least that in a changing world, where every different government may have a different sense of values, there is no guarantee whatsoever of their permanency.

There is today a tremendous international feeling that at all costs wetlands must be preserved. There is even a distinct possibility that this campaign may be more successful than many hoped, for we are just about to discover that any virtue that may accrue from over-drainage of land is being more than offset by the acute shortage of water which has arisen in a great many countries. Fresh water is a tremendous asset, yet vast sums have been spent for decades in countries like Great Britain getting it back into the sea in the quickest possible time. If there is now a water shortage, one is bound to say that it serves us jolly well right. It seems highly likely that at least some of the hundreds of thousands of acres of good food-producing agricultural land in England would not have had to be submerged under the waters of artificial reservoirs if our water resources had been properly planned. It is fashionable to have a dig at planners who after all are usually only trying to do a job of work to the best of their ability and who suffer from being put into departmental blinkers: the fact that planning in most countries has been a remarkable overall failure is surely due in the main to the fact that there has been no proper co-ordination.

This problem of drainage could completely destroy, for instance, a reserve like Minsmere in Suffolk; not drainage on the reserve itself, of course, but operations higher up the sources from which the fresh water comes might cut off the vital supply. If this happened, the whole reserve, at least as far as the marshland was concerned, would collapse and all the work and expense over the years brought to nought. If anyone should happen to think that no self-respecting government would allow this sort of thing to happen, then he should take a look at history.

One of the most famous of all wetland nature reserves is the Everglades in Florida, a vast area of semi-tropical swamp through which water slowly seeps away down to the sea from a large lake away to the north. This is a paradise for birds, many of which are uncommon or rare, as well as harbouring many other interesting swamp-loving creatures such as alligators. But it now appears that the whole project is in jeopardy as a result of the demand for water and the tapping of the supply from the lake which feeds the Everglades. At the moment of writing this in the summer of 1965 much of the swampy area has apparently become completely dry and the alligators and other creatures for whom the water is essential are dying on the sun-baked mud. Pathetic enough in itself, this sort of thing bodes ill for the whole future of conservation. Wherever protection is thought of almost any-where in the world, the Everglades sanctuary is known and admired by repute and is an ornament to the American nation. And yet, apparently with all the resources of the greatest modern state, even if they have not lost it entirely, it begins to look as if this fantastic reserve will never be the same again.

If a great and wealthy nation cannot adequately conserve its wild life, it might well be asked what can be expected of some of the smaller countries. In fact some of the smaller ones do remarkably well. The Netherlands is an excellent example, for with a relatively small land area and an extremely high density of population they have so far succeeded in holding their own if not surpassing almost any other Euro-pean country. However, the Netherlands has one great advantage over a country like Britain in that they are much better able to control access. In Great Britain there is a tremendous open air movement (with which I am in great sympathy) and ramblers and everybody else insist upon the right to walk over moorlands, mountains and the seashore. I am not blaming them, for I have enjoyed doing much the same thing. Recreational demands have got to be met. But is it essential that we should be able to walk over every square yard of our heritage? If more areas of the foreshore, but only a fraction of the whole, could be marked off and kept free from trippers, terns and other sea birds could not only be given a better chance of survival but they would also add to the pleasures of at least the more observant holiday-makers.

It was disturbing, if symptomatic of the intolerant and selfish age in which we live, to read in the Proceedings of the Study Conference on 'The Countryside in 1970', held in London in November 1963, these words from the representative of the Ramblers' Association: 'There was still much opposition to townsmen in the countryside, but one

8

could not cage four-fifths of the population in the towns nor could one canalize them along selected tracks.' Provided that there are a reasonable number of tracks, canalisation of that kind is precisely what one ought to do in wilderness country, otherwise it and its wild life will be destroyed. Go to the right places, and no rambler need find things overcrowded, even if he does keep to conventional tracks. Just over a year ago, together with the Editor of these 'Survival books', I walked from Speyside along the path through the Llarig Ghru, that yawning divide in the high Cairngorms, on down beside the Dee and then, crossing over it, we went down the track through the whole length of Glen Tilt into Blair Atholl. We did this forty-mile stretch in one go. For over thirty miles, which took us fifteen hours, we never saw another living soul, even though it was midsummer.

Access certainly: but not 'access to excess' unless we are going to be selfish and foolish enough to destroy the very thing we seek. The Cairngorm mountains, probably the finest range of hills in Britain, are already imperilled. The easiest way to get on to the high tops there has probably always been to climb up the long but gentle slope of Cairngorm. Until fairly recently one could get a car only as far as the east end of Loch Morlich, near Glenmore Lodge. Most people were put off by the four-mile climb to the summit and many of those who did essay it had had enough when they got to the top, simply enjoying the view and then returning. But in 1959 the side of the mountain was scarred by a motor-road which leads up to a car park at 3,000 feet. Soon afterwards a ski-lift was erected. So far as the winter sports were concerned, little or no harm was done to the wild life of the area, though some fine scenery was desecrated. But, as the object behind the exercise was to make money, the ski-lift was used in summer to take those who had motored up to the car-park on up to the summit at seven and a tanner a time. So greatly increased numbers of people now get on to Cairngorm quickly and without any great exertion. They have both the time and the strength to go wandering over the lovely plateau towards Ben Macdhui, disturbing the dotterel and other rare wild life.

Granted that the economy of the Highlands of Scotland is in a poor way. Much of what is being done is no doubt for the common good.

Nor is it reasonable to sneer at profit motives. We are all engaged in making money; even conservationists do not work for nothing. Nor is there any valid reason to suppose that those who are behind developments such as those going ahead in the Cairngorms are oblivious to the beauty of this almost unspoilt part of the British heritage. The trouble is that, once the machinery of development is started up, nobody seems to be able to control it and the next generation, for whom we are everlastingly promising so much, will be left wringing their hands at our short-sighted ineptitude.

We cannot save all wild places nor all the wild life of the world. But this offers no excuse whatsoever for not taking adequate steps to save all that we can. I am reminded of a very pertinent remark made by Mr Jack Longland at the 'Countryside in 1970' Conference: 'I suppose yesterday's conference emphasised (as in fact most of the other background papers have done) that very curious paradox of the English, that they combine a perfectly genuine passion for the countryside with an almost unequalled skill in destroying it.'

All too much of the destruction of wild life arises quite unwittingly. The naturalists are protesting at the colossal destruction of old hedges which is at present going on in most agricultural districts of Britain and in many other countries as well. By breaking up the soil and exposing a food-supply, agricultural practices have probably greatly increased the total number of birds, though not necessarily the variety of species. But if the birds can find food, many of them must have the hedgerow cover for nesting. So the grubbing up of hedges is, from the conservationist's point of view, highly undesirable. Yet farming is an essential industry and modern machinery has made the old-fashioned small field uneconomic. By clearing some of his hedges, the farmer can convert half a dozen fields into one unit which is, for him, much more effective. Nobody can blame him for doing so; at least, not if they are reasonable people. But cannot farmers be persuaded to keep those hedgerows which do divide his larger fields in proper order? Not if you keep on abusing him, as far too many naturalists are apt to do.

Farmers have even become something of an Aunt Sally in the uproar which has developed over the use of highly toxic poisons in husbandry. Lethal substances, of some sort or another, have been in use for a very long time in the service of crop protection. But since the end of the Second World War, first in the United States and then in Britain and elsewhere, the practice of spreading more and more poisons on the land, with little regard to the ultimate consequences, has become very big business indeed. Many of these chemicals are remarkably persistent, remaining more or less unchanged in the soil for years and getting into ditches and drains, and so into rivers and lakes and, ultimately, into the sea. Unless this sort of thing can be brought under control, the future of many forms of our flora and fauna simply does not bear thinking about. That most of the manufacturers of these products are very much to blame for the present situation is almost certainly true. Without any study of the possible side-effects (including effects on human beings, too) most of them repeatedly issued pledges that their products were really quite harmless and that the misgivings of the naturalists were nothing more than a lot of sentimental ballyhoo. It is little consolation, that, little by little and at considerable expense, the conservationists are exposing many of these claims to be misleading: in fact, I do not think that fraudulent would be an unfair term to use.

Some of the most persistent of these poisons, in the chlorinated hydrocarbon group, are slowly being withdrawn. But, as I have shown in a previous book in this series, *Birds of Prey*, the harm which they have already done has been nothing less than a disastrous setback to conservation: much of the damage may be irreparable. But, as governments are at least supposed to control things on behalf of the nations, the ultimate responsibility cannot be laid on the shoulders of the manufacturers although, as far as Britain is concerned, both parties might not be ill-advised if they gave some of their highly paid scientific advisers the sack.

All over the world, for one reason and another, birds of prey seem to be on the way out. Many of them, like the vultures and kites, are scavengers and the more hygienic mankind becomes the more difficult will it be for such birds to peck a living as civilisation encroaches into the remaining wildernesses. Other birds of prey are destroyed because they interfere, either actually or in the imagination, with the welfare of domestic animals. Many are destroyed by ignorance or prejudice. But probably never before in history have so many of this fine group of birds been destroyed or rendered infertile than in the few years since persistent poisons were showered over the land as if nothing else mattered but killing. It is only necessary to study the recent disastrous breeding seasons of the osprey in the United States of America to realise precisely what is going on.

Though the foolish and shortsighted use of persistent poisons has had a disastrous effect on birds of prey in many lands during the last twenty years, this magnificent group of birds, numerically relatively small, has always been under pressure. Only with the utmost difficulty has it been possible to preserve a reasonable population of the golden eagle in Scotland. The birds have been shot on a scale which has made nonsense of protective legislation and their eggs have been taken by selfish, shortsighted collectors. But this wanton dissipation of a heritage which is far, far older in its occupation of the world than even the most primitive of men is not by any means confined to Europe and North America. Illustrations in this book show the likely fate of the wedgetailed eagle, a noble relative of the golden eagle, which is found in Australia. Wedge-tails are disliked by sheep-farmers and possibly they may occasionally kill young lambs. But it is as well to bear in mind that wanton destruction of the irreplaceable on this scale is something which has only been practised by civilised man in modern times.

Yet in the very midst of this holocaust in the natural world, when the pessimistic person might be justified in wondering whether there is any purpose in struggling on, we read that a boy has been fined £4 for illegally shooting one of Britain's commonest birds with an air-gun. When this sort of thing is advertised as a sort of minor triumph in the cause of bird protection, it is difficult to be optimistic.

The suppression of animals, mainly insects (numerically speaking, at least), which may seriously damage the interests of man, his health and his crops, ought to be admitted as necessary and desirable in a world which is still largely ridden with hunger and disease. Yet, apart from the fact that many pesticides destroy the beneficial along with the harmful, what happens to many birds if, say, the majority of flies are going to be annihilated? Flycatchers must have flies to catch. There is in the north of Iceland a very famous laval lake, Myvatn, which is almost fantastically rich in its breeding population of a huge variety of duck, as well as phalaropes and other birds. Now the word Myvatn, in Icelandic, means midges and it was so named because midges absolutely swarm there in the summer. In a recent article in the *Shooting Times*, Dr Jeffery Harrison described a visit to Myvatn. The whole lake appeared to be smoking as the flies danced in clouds over the water. Swimming duck left a clear passage for a few yards behind them between the scum which was, in fact, formed by dead insects.

The midges of Myvatn are real biters. They make life unpleasant for human beings, amongst other creatures. But they form a fantastic food supply for an almost fantastic number of birds. Clean them all up (if you can) and you may make life much more pleasant for the visitor to Myvatn. But, in doing so, you may clean up most of the rich variety of wild life which makes this lake a positive Mecca for European ornithologists. Sooner or later (and unless it is pretty soon it may well be too late anyway) man has got to learn that he cannot have it both ways. Like any other creature, he must learn to give as well as to take. He sits astride the top of the pyramid of evolution, the most intelligent, the most capable of all the creatures in the animal kingdom. Does he just kick like a donkey and go to the devil or does he use his powers of tolerance and understanding to enable him and his successors to see the brightness of the skirts of God?

Index